First Lady, Public Wife

First Lady, Public Wife

A behind-the-scenes history of the evolving role of First Ladies in American political life

JAMES S. ROSEBUSH

Madison
★ BOOKS ★

Lanham   New York   London

Copyright © 1987 by James S. Rosebush

Madison Books
4720 Boston Way
Lanham, MD 20706

3 Henrietta Street
London WC2E 8LU England

Printed in the United States of America
91   90   89   88   87   5   4   3   2   1

To my loving wife Nancy and my dear daughters
Claire and Lauren

Library of Congress Cataloging-in-Publication Data

Rosebush, James S.
First lady, public wife.

1. Presidents — United States — Wives.   I. Title.
E176.2.R67   1987   973.09'92   87-24051
ISBN 0-8191-6497-6

British Cataloging in Publication Information Available

Designed by Meadows & Wiser, Washington, D.C.

Text composed in Caslon 540 by General Typographers,
Inc., Washington, D.C. Typositor in Caslon 540 by Phil's
Photo, Inc., Washington, D.C.

Printed by R. R. Donnelley & Sons Company, Willard,
Ohio.

Frontispiece: President and Mrs. Reagan walk in the
garden at Maison de Saussure, their residence during the
Geneva Summit, November 1985.

Contents

Preface

American society — its ethics, goals, drives, and even how it identifies itself — seems to be always changing. This constant evolution is often reflected in shifting political trends and platforms and in the public's expectations of political candidates and elected government officials. Constitutional authority and historical and legal precedent fix the role of the President of the United States, but the role of the presidential spouse is more affected by shifts in social trends and more subject to a wide range of critical interpretation by the public and by the individuality of the First Lady herself. As the public awareness and visibility of the First Lady has increased, public scrutiny and debate over the job and her job performance has increased dramatically.

It is into this freewheeling but increasingly important debate that I interject a few of my own observations. I have seen the inner workings of the White House at close range. I began working on President Reagan's staff in 1981 and then served as chief of staff for First Lady Nancy Reagan from 1982 to 1986. While working for the First Lady, I maintained my position as Deputy Assistant to the President. From this unique vantage point, I observed a growing interrelationship between the East and West Wings of the White House and I helped provide a link between the staff of the President and that of First Lady. This growing cooperation between the two staffs itself may reflect a subtly different and more active role for the First Lady in American political life.

In this book I will share some of the insights I gained from my experience in the White House, briefly discuss how the duties of the First Lady have evolved, and examine the interpretation of the role by various First Ladies including Nancy Reagan. Numerous biographies of First Ladies exist, but very little has been written about the job of First Lady. My interest is not in the biographical details of First Ladies, which are best left to historians, but in the political ramifications of what I see as an expanding role for the most important political spouse in the world. Perhaps we are even heading toward a legislative or legal definition of the role. How fixed this job definition becomes will be largely dependent upon the next two or three spouses — the spouses who follow Nancy Reagan.

Although I realize some public criticism has attempted to trivialize the position of First Lady, in looking back at my experience with Mrs. Reagan, I began to delineate the specific, public expectations of the job and saw that the position is extremely complicated and difficult. Public polls often judge presidents on "job performance." Can the exact same criteria apply for his or her spouse, especially when few people can agree on the job description?

I have attempted, in this book, to bring better definition to the job and to discuss how First Ladies throughout history have interpreted it and performed in it. I have tried to judge the dimensions of the job so that future First Lady observers will be in a better position to rate job performance.

It is with this in mind I divided the job into six functions or categories and I have based my writing on these. The six functions follow: manager, diplomat, hostess, champion of causes, political partner, wife and mother.

I am grateful to have had an opportunity to observe, at close range, one woman's interpretation of the job. Aside from whether or not Nancy Reagan is judged by history as an effective Public Wife, my association with her was a fascinating learning experience in American politics, public issues, public opinion, and press and media relations. Nancy Reagan and others I worked closely with in government were effective teachers, but in the end, it was the turn of events themselves and how they were anticipated and handled that was most instructive. In this perspective, every foreign trip, every drug briefing, every press interview, every meeting, every social event taught me something that is now woven into an experience I will always value.

The role of the First Lady has ranged from the strictly private to active involvement. Nancy Reagan blends both aspects: her concern for her husband's well-being and her dedication to the anti-drug campaign.

First Lady Firsts

Abigail Adams was the first First Lady to live at 1600 Pennsylvania Avenue.

Martha Jefferson Randolph, Thomas Jefferson's daughter and acting First Lady, was the first to give birth to a child in the White House.

Dolley Madison was the only First Lady ever awarded a place of honor in Congress.

Louisa Adams was the only foreign-born First Lady.

Rachel Jackson was the only First Lady to smoke pipes and cigars.

Anna Harrison was the first First Lady to be awarded a pension from Congress upon her husband's death.

Priscilla Cooper Tyler was the first professional actress to serve as First Lady.

Julia Tyler was the first First Lady to marry an incumbent president.

Abigail Fillmore was the first First Lady to earn her own living before marriage.

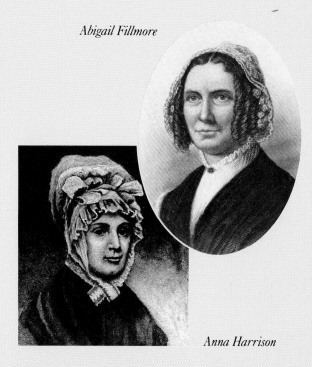

Abigail Fillmore

Anna Harrison

Frances Cleveland was the first First Lady to be married in the White House.

Frances Cleveland was the first First Lady to remarry after her husband, the former President, had died.

Helen Taft was the first First Lady to order and ride in an automobile.

Ellen Wilson was the first First Lady whose special project became Congressional legislation.

Edith Wilson was the first to travel overseas during her time as First Lady.

Florence Harding was the first divorced woman to serve as First Lady.

Grace Coolidge was the first incumbent First Lady to vote.

Grace Coolidge was the first First Lady to receive an honorary college degree.

Grace Coolidge was the first First Lady to smoke cigarettes.

Lou Hoover was the first First Lady to deliver speeches over the radio.

Abigail Adams

Eleanor Roosevelt was the first First Lady to hold formal press conferences.

Eleanor Roosevelt was the first to fly by airplane as First Lady.

Eleanor Roosevelt was the first First Lady to be given an official government position — Assistant Director, Office of Civil Defense — during her husband's term.

Eleanor Roosevelt was the first First Lady to make public speeches on a regular basis.

Bess Truman was the first First Lady to install air conditioning in the White House.

Jacqueline Kennedy was the first First Lady to give a television tour of the White House.

Lady Bird Johnson was the first First Lady to go on the campaign trail for her husband on her own, targeting one region of the country.

Lady Bird Johnson was the only First Lady to own her own radio station.

Nancy Reagan and Jacqueline Kennedy Onassis

Pat Nixon was the first First Lady to represent her husband at the inauguration of a foreign leader.

Pat Nixon was the first First Lady to have appeared in motion pictures before she was First Lady.

Pat Nixon was the first First Lady to have the mansion illuminated at night for the public.

Betty Ford was the first First Lady to appear on a television sitcom while First Lady.

Rosalynn Carter was the first First Lady to attend Cabinet meetings.

Nancy Reagan was the first incumbent First Lady to speak at the United Nations.

Nancy Reagan was the first First Lady to appear in a music video for the promotion of a project of special interest.

Nancy Reagan was the first First Lady to sing on stage on Broadway.

Nancy Reagan was the first First Lady to hold a meeting on a single substantive issue with a Pope.

Nancy Reagan was the first First Lady to host an international conference for first ladies from around the world.

Lou Hoover

Florence Harding

First Lady: By Popular Demand

She's not elected, she's not paid a salary, she has no constitutional authority or statutory duties and she can't be impeached. She inherits her position solely by marriage. Individual character and the winds of popular opinion change the job description with every new presidential administration. The women who have filled the position have had distinctly individualistic styles. Their average age has been forty-seven, most have been Episcopalians and more have been born in New York than any other state in the Union. The only facts that even remotely draw them together as a group are that all of them served as hostess for the President of the United States.

In recent history, the role of First Lady has been performed by the President's wife. But other women, in some way related to the President, have often acted as surrogate First Ladies. For example, Elizabeth Monroe, President Monroe's wife, was often in poor health so she shared the role of First Lady with her daughter, Eliza Hay. When John Tyler came into the presidency, his ailing wife, Letitia, managed the private entertaining in the family quarters while her daughter-in-law Priscilla served as the official First Lady. When Letitia Tyler died and Priscilla moved to Philadelphia, Tyler's daughter Letitia Semple served as First Lady for four months. Then, the President married Julia Gardiner; so, four different women acted as First Lady during Tyler's single term.

In all, fifty-one women, either wives or other relatives, have performed the role of presidential hostess. Thirty-six First Ladies were married to Presidents. Seven women who were married to men who served as president of the United States never served as First Lady. Five of them — Martha Jefferson, Rachel Jackson, Hannah Van Buren, Ellen Arthur, and Alice Roosevelt — did not live to see their husbands assume office. Two others, Caroline Fillmore and Mary Lord Harrison, married after their husbands had completed their terms of office.

*O*n "First Lady's Night," Nancy Reagan looks out on a sea of enthusiastic delegates to the 1984 Republican Convention. She closed by calling for "four more years for the gipper."

*D*olley Madison, a practised hostess, having assisted widower Thomas Jefferson before becoming First Lady herself, became a legend. Well-loved and respected, she set a standard her successors were hard put to match.

pleted their terms of office.

Only two bachelors have ever been elected President, Buchanan and Cleveland. James Buchanan's niece, Harriet Lane, served as his hostess. Cleveland married while living in the executive mansion. His sister Rose served as First Lady until he wed Frances Folsom. William Henry Harrison's wife Anna was too ill to travel with him to Washington but historians often count her among the First Ladies. Two others also acted as First Lady during Harrison's one short month in the White House — the President's daughter-in-law Jane Irwin Harrison and her aunt Jane Findlay.

Six presidential couples have been childless: the Washingtons, the Madisons, the Jacksons, the Polks, Woodrow Wilson and his second wife, and the Hardings. Except for the Polks, however, each couple had children from a previous marriage or by adoption. George Washington adopted Martha Washington's two children by her first marriage and during his presidency the Washingtons raised two of her grandchildren as their own. James Madison adopted Dolley Madison's son Payne by her marriage to lawyer John Todd. Andrew and Rachel Jackson legally adopted one of her nephews, and named him Andrew Jackson, Jr. His wife Sarah Yorke Jackson served as one of President Jackson's two White House hostesses. Warren Harding supported Peter De Wolfe, his wife Florence's son from her first marriage, but the young man died before his mother became First Lady. Children who were raised in the White House, or who lived or visited there as adults always enlivened

*J*acqueline Kennedy examines with architect John Warnecke the plans for the proposed restoration of Lafayette Square opposite the White House. The original 19th century buildings had been slated for demolition.

*F*our generations of the Benjamin Harrison family filled the executive mansion to overflowing. Here daughter-in-law, Mrs. Russel Harrison, and grandchildren stand near the North Portico.

the gossip about presidential families and, depending on an individual's point of view and the discipline of the presidential children, either complicated or complemented the lives of the Presidents during their terms.

No one knows precisely where the title First Lady came from. It was prominently used for the first time when reporter Mary Clemmer Ammes, writing about the 1877 inauguration of Rutherford Hayes, referred to Lucy Webb Hayes as "the First Lady of the land." By the time Grover Cleveland's much heralded White House wedding took place in June 1886, the title had become permanently affixed to the presidential wife or official hostess. Not too many spouses, however, have felt really comfortable being called First Lady. Jacqueline Kennedy, for one, thought it sounded more like a name for a racehorse than a title for a person and she asked that it not be used.

Martha Washington, who preferred the privacy of family to the demands of public life, must have been called by names more suited to royalty than a frontier woman. Abigail Adams was called "Mrs. President" and sometimes referred to as "Her Majesty." Dolley Madison, who had a long reign in Washington society even before her husband became President, was simply called "Lady Presidentess."

One thing seems clear: whatever the title, the women who have functioned as First Lady were all thrown into the job with little preparation for the tremendous responsibilities that fall on the spouse of the most powerful public office-holder in the world. Even the most experienced political campaigners have been surprised, once their husbands were elected, by the lack of personal and family privacy and the multiple demands that came with their husbands' new office. Most presidential spouses have filled the new role effectively and responded with a sense of duty, but there is no single standard by which

*B*etty Ford holds her first press conference in the East Room. During her relatively short "term," she discussed with
unusual openness and warmth personal experiences and opinions about her family and her health problems.

to judge the performance of the whole group. Each woman has given a unique definition to the role. Political affiliation and party platform can result in a predictable performance by a President, but his wife, with no political or legal blueprint, can write her own job description. Sometimes this is a troublesome liability for her husband, sometimes it is an asset.

Good health, education, determination, and the demands of the depression and World War II made Eleanor Roosevelt a tremendous asset to an often wheelchair-bound President, though she was not without controversy. Betty Ford's outspokenness was at first considered damaging to her husband's administration. But public reaction turned from severe criticism to sympathy as she shared her personal health problems with the public. Finally, she emerged as a bona fide asset during the Ford years.

*M*artha Washington, our country's first First Lady,
faced the problem of defining a role for a position
which had never been filled before. Her formal receptions
hinted at the influence of royalty. (overleaf)

Rosalynn Carter contributed to her husband's policy formation and was criticized for exerting too much influence on government programs. Nancy Reagan turned an image that could have been a disastrous political liability into one that ultimately added to her husband's popularity.

What do Americans really want in their First Lady? Today, with the evolving role of women in the workplace, the rising expectations placed on women in society, the increasing degree to which women are involved in substantive decision-making from household management to foreign policy, the duties of the First Lady have changed dramatically. No more is she just an official hostess for the White House. Recent presidential marriages have reflected contemporary views of what is an acceptable sharing of responsibilities between married partners. For example, it is more commonplace today for men to consult their wives on a wide range of issues. Publicly, women's opinions are no longer restricted to domestic affairs, but are sought out in all fields.

In the future, with more women pursuing careers outside the home, we can expect that the

*P*rime Minister Margaret Thatcher greets the Reagans in 1983 during their visit to England for the Economic
Summit. The First Lady can help cement good relations with foreign leaders.

wife of a President might choose to pursue her own legal practice or writing career or education instead of focusing exclusively on the official duties of First Lady. She might even reject some official responsibilities in favor of things she considers more important personally, such as the care of her family, or to follow a career which she feels would more effectively contribute to society. In France, Italy, Sweden, the Soviet Union, and doubtless other countries, some first ladies have already chosen to continue their professional careers. For example, we are led to believe that Raisa Gorbachev, though she has a good deal of interest in politics, has continued to teach at the University of Moscow. Anna Craxi continued to work in Milan during her husband's tenure as Italy's prime minister, commuting to Rome for official functions. Danielle Mitterrand also decided not to give up her career when her husband was elected president of France.

It is probable that in the future Americans will elect a woman President. Although few other political systems mirror that of the United States, one can see a parallel in the experience of Denis Thatcher. Although he has been a staunch supporter of his wife, Margaret, the prime minister, he has chosen a decidedly different role than Americans might envision for a "First Husband." I remember vividly the discussions we had with the British foreign secretary's office when Mrs. Reagan invited first ladies from around the world to participate in a first-time-ever world conference of first ladies on drug abuse. Would Denis Thatcher attend? Should the title of the conference be changed to reflect all first spouses? After lengthy and rather delicate conversations with British officials we learned that Mr. Thatcher would prefer not to be invited and not to be cast in the role of a crusading first lady. Had he attended Mrs. Reagan's conference, it would have caused quite a stir, more than the British or Americans wanted to handle so he probably made the right decision. Although Denis Thatcher has been the subject of many cartoons and caricatures, he has developed a role in which he is comfortable and which the British people generally seem to accept. The fact remains, however, that in the future the issue of gender in this supporting role in any country will require more unconventional solutions.

First Ladies have typically reflected the behavior and social mores of their generation and the political demands of the time and while this has been true, it is also true that their own individual character traits, education, and family background also prevailed. For example, while Mary Todd Lincoln, rising to the demands of the times, went into the field to nurse Civil War casualties, she also saw her lavish wardrobe and entertainments as ways to help keep northern industry alive. Lou Hoover also used clothing as a national statement. She chose to wear all cotton to boost the cotton industry which was badly affected by the depression. Earlier, both President and Mrs. Washington had dressed exclusively in American-made clothing to make a political statement and to show a decided personal preference.

Some First Ladies were quick to boost technology as it became available. Sarah Polk brought gas lighting into the White House; Caroline Harrison, electricity. Grace Coolidge loved the radio and kept it blaring away in the White House family quarters. Eleanor Roosevelt enjoyed flying, and she was often photographed boarding a flight. The Eisenhowers helped popularize television, often having their dinner on TV trays while watching a western or comedy.

On a more serious note, First Ladies have been quick to pick up on cause-related movements. For example, during World War I, Edith Wilson abided gasless Sundays and meatless Mondays. Many First Ladies have led bond drives. Lucy Hayes's ban on liquor reflected the abstinence movement of the 1870s. Betty Ford's openness on social issues reflected a national trend toward more candor on personal matters.

Sometimes First Ladies made causes of the public issues of their day. Jacqueline Kennedy gave the historic preservation movement a substantial boost and Lady Bird Johnson championed beautification programs. Today, both of these movements are substantial and accepted as everyday aspects of American culture.

But in actuality no job description exists for First Lady, and the American people are often undecided as to what that role should be. They seem to want a First Lady who is just as comfortable scrubbing the floor in a pair of blue jeans as attending a formal ball at Windsor Castle in an American designer gown.

People want to idealize their First Lady, but they don't want her to idealize herself. They want her to work on causes but to save enough energy to entertain impeccably, speak foreign languages, travel comfortably (but inexpensively), and maintain a happy homelife. And, what's more, they are ready to criticize severely any First Lady who cannot perform well in most of these functions or any First Lady who oversteps in the interpretation of her role. After all, "we didn't *elect* a First Lady," they will tell you.

Americans seem to have a hard time agreeing on the ideal First Lady. In 1985, when Mrs. Reagan's public acceptance reached an all-time high, the man in the street was asked why she was so popular. The responses were somewhat surprising. The reasons most often mentioned were decidedly diverse: her dedication to a cause as serious and far-reaching as drug abuse and her constant support of her husband. It is easy to understand widespread admiration for work on a societal problem found in one of every three American households; but the second reason shows a continuing thread of conservatism in American values. For a wife to support her husband with Nancy Reagan's fervency and attention is not an image popularized in society today. These polls show that underneath popular trends there must be a value system that is much more traditional than what is portrayed by the media.

While the public liked Nancy Reagan's dedication to her husband, they criticized her whenever she crossed a fine line into what is called "pushiness" or "control." Popular opinion says to First Ladies, "You must support the

Eleanor Roosevelt set out to show that airline travel could be safe and acceptable for a lady. As First Lady she travelled the world for her wheelchair-bound husband and to crusade for her own beliefs and causes.

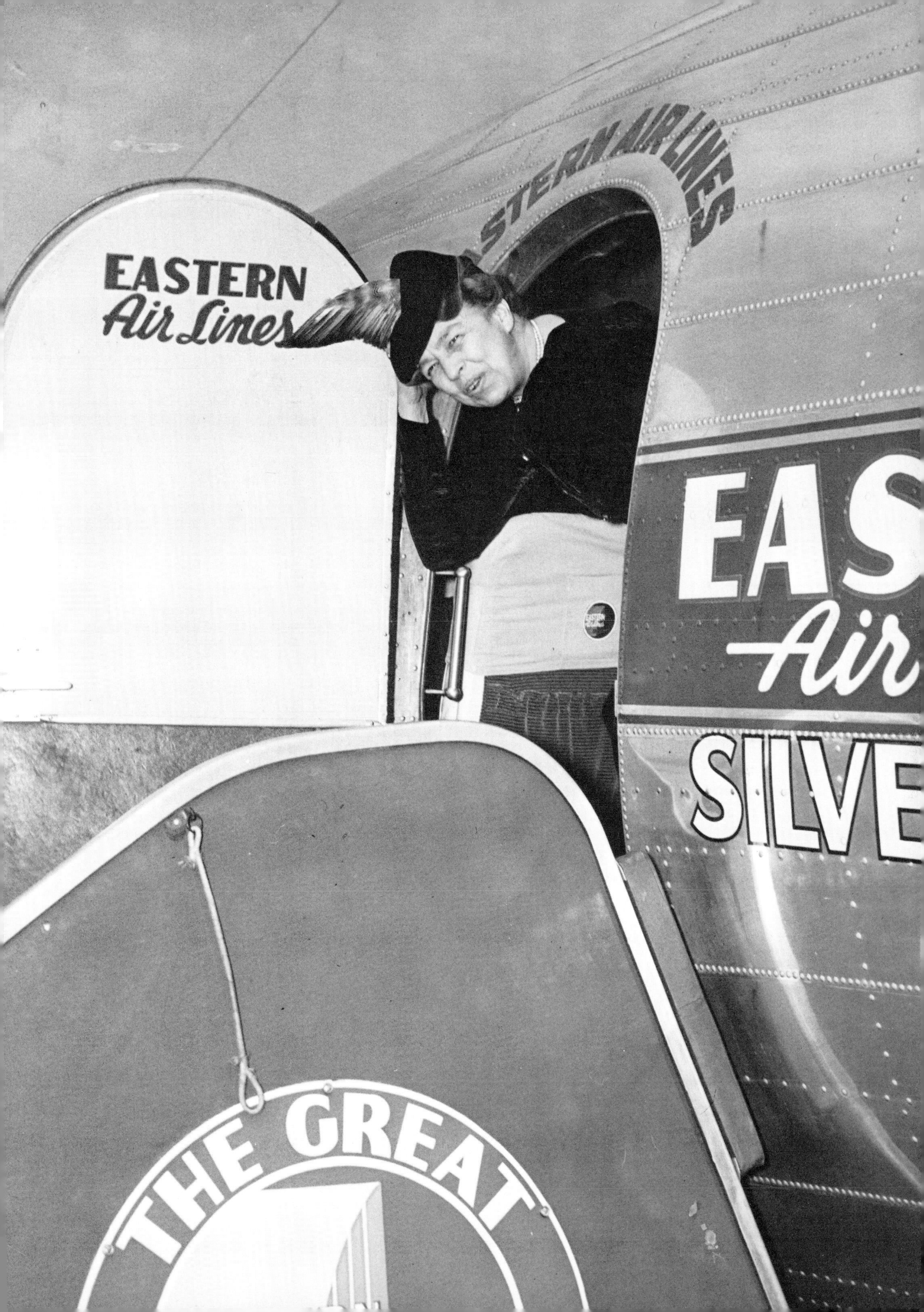
EASTERN
Air Lines
STERN AIRLINES
EAS
Air
SILVE
THE GREAT

*T*wo *First Ladies, one present, one future: Pat Nixon as Vice-Presidential wife joins Mamie Eisenhower, the*
President's wife in celebrating Mrs. Eisenhower's 63rd birthday. Both interpreted their role in a traditional way.

President. Advise him in the quiet of your own quarters, but allow him to make his own decisions." In the uproar over the departure of the President's chief of staff Donald Regan, Nancy Reagan was almost crucified as a meddling, power-hungry woman of mad ambition. Ambition? Certainly. But an important distinction was lost in the debate. Nancy Reagan's ambition — unlike that of Edith Wilson, Julia Tyler, or perhaps even Eleanor Roosevelt — was not for herself but resulted from a built-in defense mechanism that surfaced when her husband was threatened. Earlier, Nancy Reagan tested that invisible barrier when she spoke, under her breath to the President, in answer to a question shouted to him by a nearby news correspondent. While her instinctive reaction may have been

that of most people in the same situation, she received a strong rebuke from the media — a rebuke which, I think, led her to exercise even greater restraint and caution when she is in the public eye. For the most part, though, Nancy Reagan has followed a stay-in-the-background dictum. Future husband-wife teams may interpret their own interrelationships, however, in ways that could test the public's tolerance of what they think is acceptable between the President and his "closest advisor."

It is also possible that a man could be elected or not elected President because of the popularity of his spouse. Political advisors today are quick to judge the media value of potential political candidates and their spouses. If the wife appears to be a handicap in winning popular support, the candidate may be advised to stay out of politics.

In the summer of 1960 when reporters began to write about Jacqueline Kennedy's fashionable image, many in the campaign feared it might be a liability. The Nixon advisors saw this as an opportunity to promote the Republican cloth-coat image associated with Pat Nixon. The Kennedy campaigners' fears never materialized. During Eisenhower's campaign, rumors were circulated that Mamie was an alcoholic; but again the potential liability bore no fruit. These problems mirrored an earlier time when a First Lady was the target of political slander. In 1896, Ida McKinley was charged with insanity; others thought she was a spy. The truth was that Mrs. McKinley suffered from epilepsy and remained in the background through most of the presidential campaign. Ida's precarious health and her husband's devotion to her, however, won him sympathetic support by the time of the campaign of 1900.

Three First Ladies had divorces which became campaign issues: Rachel Jackson, Florence Harding, and Betty Ford. Mrs. Jackson's divorce was a major issue in her husband's campaign and cartoons and editorials pictured her as a bigamist. Florence Harding gave reporters an earlier year as the date of her first husband's death in an attempt to portray herself as a widow instead of a divorcée. Divorce was an issue in the campaigns of Gerald Ford and of Nelson Rockefeller. But by the time the Reagans were campaigning, Ronald Reagan's previous marriage, while discussed openly, was not the issue it had been in previous campaigns.

Although Nancy Reagan was not totally comfortable appearing on her own in the 1976 or 1980 presidential campaigns, she became such an energetic campaigner in 1984 that some political observers have called her the perfect political wife.

Any First Lady must be, according to public dictates, attentive and interested in anyone — farmers, factory workers, and kings — but not too familiar. She must be well informed about her husband's political agendas, regardless of her interest in them. She is expected to reflect the spirit of America — the whole country — without regard to her own regional background. She must treat the press without contempt, even though they can treat her with it. Be well dressed, not overdressed. Be prepared, not rehearsed. Be a devoted wife, but also a woman of independence. Express opinions frankly, but never be flippant. Care for the house, but never appear too absorbed in it. Show emotion, but never appear contrived. Is it any wonder that Margaret Truman once called the position of First Lady "the second hardest job in America"?

Lady Bird Johnson came well-prepared for the role of First Lady in part because of the business training she had received from her father. She had helped her husband during his years in Congress and the Vice Presidency.

The Working First Lady

Martha Washington, writing from Philadelphia, then our nation's capital, described public life there as almost an agony for her. "I live a very dull life here," she wrote, "and know nothing that passes in the town — I never go to any public places — indeed, I think I am more like a state prisoner than anything else, and there are certain bounds set for me which I must not depart from. . . ."

Her successor, Abigail Adams, though more outspoken and active in public life, revealed the same kind of revulsion to demands placed on her. She wrote, "I'm. . .sick, sick of public life. . .if my future peace and tranquility were all that I considered, a release from public life would be the most desirable event of it."

Louisa Adams, wife of John Quincy Adams, found her life in the White House like that of "a bird in a cage" and felt lonely and melancholy.

After her battle with a press corps that severely criticized her for excessive spending and ostentation, Mary Todd Lincoln began to lose the lighter, happier mood which characterized her first two years in the White House. After one severe critic handed her an especially sharp attack, she wrote, "Oh! It is no use to make any defense; all such efforts would only make me a target for new attacks. I do not belong to the public; my character is wholly domestic, and the public have nothing to do with it."

Jane Pierce found the White House so overwhelming that she did not appear as public hostess for the first two years of her husband's administration. Mrs. Pierce suffered from tuberculosis and Washington's damp climate worsened her condition. As a congressional wife she had fled the capital for that very reason. She also despised politicians and was condescending to them.

Martha Patterson, the daughter of Andrew Johnson who served as public hostess, told the press that she and her family were "plain people

O nly two months before her husband's inauguration, Jane Pierce saw her 11-year-old son, Benny, above, killed in a railway accident. Her grief, coupled with her tuberculosis, severely limited her activities.

from the mountains of Tennessee" and she hoped that "not too much will be expected of us."

The basic unattractiveness of the young nation's capital, its damp climate, and the early uncertainties of the government probably contributed to the foreboding and doom with which the early First Ladies assessed their prospects for happiness. Abigail Adams assumed the role with a heavy heart and empty purse. Her greatest fear was the financial strain that the office would place on the family's private savings. Public entertaining was not paid for by the government and the nation's hostess often found herself short of cash.

Martha Washington called her years as First Lady the "lost years" and desperately feared

N ancy Reagan receives thousands of letters a month. Here she reviews some of the many heart-breaking letters she received about drug abuse while talking to a mother who is trying to help her daughter.

T he only First Lady not born in America, Louisa Adams preferred quiet activities such as winding the silk from silkworms she had reared, but she was an outstanding hostess nevertheless. (overleaf)

their effect on the grandchildren they were raising. Margaret Taylor's reluctance to serve was due to her many, many years of military travel and moving with her husband, General Zachary Taylor. She had hoped their retirement would be peaceful and she bitterly resented a job she instinctively knew would kill her husband. Anna Harrison had similar fears and she was ultimately too ill to go to Washington for the Inauguration. Before her planned arrival, her husband died of pneumonia — after only one month in the presidency.

There were others who approached the new position with brighter, more accepting attitudes. Dolley Madison is one of the first who relished being First Lady, and she set a standard which several subsequent First Ladies followed. Julia Grant, Lucy Hayes, and Frances Cleveland all took some pleasure in the endless round of entertaining and caring for family and husband. As her husband was leaving office, Julia Grant wrote, "My life at the White House was a bright and beautiful dream. . . .Life at the White House was a garden spot of orchids. I wish it might have continued forever. . . ." Though less effusive, Lucy Hayes, one of the most popular First Ladies, wrote fondly of her life at the White House, but she never lost her interest in the simple homelife of Ohio. When she left the White House she wrote, "I had a particularly happy life here and yet I will hail my return home with great pleasure — four years is long enough for a woman like this one. . . .I still felt myself Lady of the House for I grew to love the house." In the face of admirers crushing in around her at receptions, Frances Cleveland's delight in the role of hostess showed in her bright smile and calm demeanor amidst the madness.

By the late 1800s the writings of First Ladies reflect a growing feeling of comfort in the job. After all, they now had role models and the public had had the opportunity to form its own opinions of what was expected of First Ladies.

One of the reasons Grace Coolidge enjoyed the job so much was that she loved people. She often quoted a musical of her time to describe the way she felt: "The old, the young, the short, the

tall, I don't give a rap, I love them all." She loved walking up to a crowd and engaging individuals in conversation. She said "people are my books." She often used her pets to encourage people to talk to her; she would often stroll on the White House grounds with Rebecca the raccoon or her white collies.

Florence Harding enjoyed nothing more than running down the grand staircase from the family quarters and surprising tourists, kissing babies, and posing for photos. Her favorite form of entertaining was the garden party and she held massive ones on the south lawn. The fountains, turned off during World War I, were ordered turned on again, the band played, and "The Duchess," as her husband called her, strolled among the crowds. Few knew that she suffered a heart and kidney ailment. She called her days as First Lady the greatest epoch of her life.

Similarly, Mamie Eisenhower tested her health and few knew that she suffered from a mild heart condition and from Ménière's disease which affected both her hearing and her equilibrium. She carried on and at public functions reporters noted that she greeted every single guest with a personal remark — asking them where they came from, and telling them how much she liked their hat or tie, or asking them about their families. As a devoted grandmother she had a special rapport with children and she reinstated the annual Easter Egg Roll which had been banned during the war and which Bess Truman had shown no interest in reviving. Mamie also insisted that every single letter sent to her receive a response, and she signed all the letters personally.

Focusing on the experiences of all thirty-six First Ladies, three patterns emerge. Some openly resented the responsibility and public scrutiny which came with the job and never felt comfortable in the role; others joyfully accepted their new position and performed well as hostess

The annual Easter Monday egg roll party held on the White House Lawn, open to all children, was started by Lucy Hayes. Here Eleanor Roosevelt joins her young guests at the party held in 1936.

and mother but never took up special causes or became close political confidants of their husbands; the third group was composed of more politically active wives who used their position to accomplish social good or achieve some political ambition for themselves or their husbands.

Most modern-day First Ladies fall into the second and third categories. Bess Truman and Mamie Eisenhower fit neatly into the second category; Eleanor Roosevelt, Lady Bird Johnson, Rosalynn Carter, and Nancy Reagan fall into the third. Jackie Kennedy and Pat Nixon seem to be hybrids, with aspects of all three groups. The First Ladies who chose active involvement in a public cause were usually rewarded with public popularity; while those who approached the job with optimism and a desire for service, not letting the situation control or change them, were rewarded with an even greater degree of success.

In earlier years, the White House did not always provide comfort for the First Ladies and their families. The building was in constant need of repair and was always understaffed. Because of this, many early First Ladies were preoccupied with simple domestic duties. Finally, beginning in 1857, Congress began to provide the funds required for the proper operation of the executive mansion. This gave a surge to the role of First Lady; it provided for a larger domestic staff and for continual refurbishment. Caroline Harrison was responsible for one early and long overdue cleaning and repairing of the White House. Her goal from the day she moved in was to have the President's house adequately cared for. She wrote, "I am very anxious to see the family of the president provided for properly, and while I am here I hope to get the present building put in good condition."

Not until the 1901 White House renovation, during the Theodore Roosevelt Administration, was a separate wing (now known as the West Wing) added for the sole purpose of housing the President's offices. Previously, the second floor of

*A*bigail Adams, the first First Lady to live in the not-yet-finished White House, spent only four months there. She wrote of the difficulties of living there, such as having to hang the laundry in the East Room.

the White House had served the dual purpose of family quarters and presidential offices. This meant a complete lack of privacy for First Families, whose rooms were grouped at the west end of the house. What is today designated as the Lincoln Bedroom once served as the Cabinet room. The formal yellow oval room, used today by First Families for entertaining, was once the presidential office. This meant — particularly in the days with fewer security requirements — that office seekers, politicians, military advisors all tramped through the family's sitting room into the hallway. Tobacco-juice stains, cigarette butts, dirty glasses, and other litter were left in the hall as if it were an office lobby. How could a First Lady expect to raise her family in privacy or seek a quiet moment from her public life? It was nearly impossible.

Providing an adequate, comfortable, and pleasant home for their husbands and families seems to have been a priority for many First Ladies. This, combined with a desire to see the public rooms of the White House well preserved, led many First Ladies into refurbishing projects. Dolley Madison, Elizabeth Monroe, Julia Tyler, Sarah Polk, Harriet Lane, Mary Lincoln, Julia Grant, Edith Roosevelt, Bess Truman, Jacqueline Kennedy, Pat Nixon, Nancy Reagan, and others all carried out redecorating plans for the state rooms and other areas.

Heavy entertainment schedules, which increased rapidly as time went by, brought wear and tear on china, silver, and glassware. Not only did table items break, but dinner guests began stealing them for souvenirs. The china service had to be replenished regularly to maintain a semblance of uniformity. Dolley Madison, Mary Lincoln, Lucy Hayes, Caroline Harrison, Edith Roosevelt, Edith Wilson, Eleanor Roosevelt, Bess Truman, Mamie Eisenhower, Lady Bird Johnson, and Nancy Reagan all ordered state china. Some of the patterns were unique. Mary Lincoln ordered china decorated with her favorite shade of purple. Lucy Hayes had American

*A*mong other hardships endured by earlier residents at the mansion were the crowds of people who milled about — *noisy, disruptive to family life — until the West Wing office was built during Theodore Roosevelt's term.*

painter Theodore Davis design unusual scenes of wildlife for the Hayes' plates. Caroline Harrison, a gifted artist, designed her own.

These purchases were necessary but costly, and almost all were subject to ridicule. Sometimes, First Ladies went overboard as when Florence Harding had the silverware triple plated in gold. But White House china purchases have almost always been controversial. Even Mrs. Kennedy's often-hailed historical refurbishment of the state rooms and redecoration of the family quarters were not without detractors. She was adding her own mark to a house that has gone through many redecorating schemes, not to mention a total rebuilding during the Truman years. Even such items of personal preference as Mamie Eisenhower's pink carpeting or Lyndon Johnson's shower stall, both paid for by public funds, were well used and well worn by the time the next occupants moved in.

Early in 1982, when I went with White House curator Clement Conger to the warehouse where remnants and remainders of White House furniture is stored, I felt as if I were visiting a museum of bad taste. Because according to public law nothing can be discarded or sold, the warehouse was full of sad, worn, ugly, and unusable pieces — this was after Mrs. Reagan had already repaired, recovered, and pressed into service almost every suitable piece that had been purchased or collected through the years.

The White House saw little change between Mrs. Nixon's refurbishment and the Reagans' arrival and by then most of the basic plumbing and plaster work dated to the Truman renovation. Nevertheless, when Mrs. Reagan devoted a major share of her first days as First Lady to planning and restoring the family quarters using private, nongovernmental contributions, she was severely criticized. When a new china service, another gift to the White House was announced, this seemed excessive to the

A swaying chandelier caused Harry Truman to order an engineering study of the White House. It found the building "was standing up purely from habit." The Trumans moved to Blair House as reconstruction began.

Bess and Harry Truman walk up the North Portico steps on their return to the White House after the complete renovation of the mansion. It had been weakened by the many earlier piecemeal alterations.

press. Critics lost sight of the fact that through breakage and theft the White House china closet was inadequate. The White House had not one matching set of china complete enough to be used to entertain a foreign head of state.

Modernizing the White House and making it comfortable seemed almost second nature to Nancy Reagan (she called it "her nesting instinct"). Yet she found herself rapidly declining in public-opinion polls because of it. This stemmed, in part, from timing. In 1981 the Reagan political platform was built on an anti-government theme with abundant discussion of cutting the budget for "entitlement" or social welfare programs. Had the redecorating program been carried out after the First Lady was better known for her serious concerns and devotion to the antidrug crusade, the redecorating and the china announcement may have been better received.

In many ways "unpaid public servant without portfolio" accurately describes the role of the First Lady today. It is as complex, demanding, and difficult a job as any. With its diversity and various commitments, it may be more demanding in some ways than the job of President. Like the President, although of a much more modest size, the First Lady has a staff to help her plan and carry out her responsibilities. In 1978 during the Carter Administration, Congress enacted Public Law 95 – 570 which, for the first time, provided legal authority for the existence of an office to fund the administration of the White House. A specific paragraph of this law (3 USC 105e) reads, "Assistance and services . . . are authorized to be provided to the spouse of the president in connection with assistance provided by such spouse to the president in discharge of the president's duties and responsibilities." Prior to the enactment of this legislation funds for the First Lady's staff and travel were appropriated on an as-needed basis from the general budget line item for White House management.

During the Theodore Roosevelt years the practice of allocating specific nondomestic staff positions to the First Lady was initiated. Isabella Hagner James tells how this came about in her remembrances, ". . . . I received a letter from Miss Young, the children's governess, who wrote for Mrs. Roosevelt, asking if I could give her several hours daily to take charge of her personal mail. She had decided on this plan, even in her first few days, largely, I think, because several of her notes, sent to the White House to Mrs. McKinley had never been acknowledged. . . . it showed a lack of system which Mrs. Roosevelt could not countenance. A little corner in Mrs. Roosevelt's bedroom now became my daily workshop and continued so until after the house was altered when I was moved to the West End of the upper corridor." Mrs. James, the first permanent staff member assigned to a First Lady, was working as a clerk in the War Department at the time she was called upon and was detailed to her new position at the salary of $1600 a year. Eventually she became a clerk on the White House payroll.

During the Eisenhower Administration the need for an organized staff for the First Lady began to emerge. Mamie Eisenhower received thousands of letters a month and she wanted them all to be answered. In addition, the

Eisenhowers entertained a record number of foreign heads of state.

New demands were soon added to the protocol, social, and correspondence requirements of prior First Ladies. Jacqueline Kennedy brought enormous media attention to the job when she entered the White House, so the position of press secretary to the First Lady was created. The job expanded in the Johnson era as Lady Bird's beautification project got underway; that project also required another kind of staff member — a projects manager.

Pat Nixon was the first to have a bona fide advance and scheduling office, and Betty Ford had the first speech writer. By the time Rosalynn Carter arrived at the White House there was a well developed staffing pattern, and she employed a management consultant to make certain that the East Wing organization was well designed and efficient.

The First Lady's staff expanded as a result of the growing demands of the job. It has leveled off at a little more than twenty during the past several administrations. Rosalynn Carter wrote in her autobiography, *First Lady from Plains*, "I thought I would have all the staff I needed. I was wrong — Jimmy planned to cut, not add to the number of people working in the White House, and all my pleas fell on deaf ears. According to the White House personnel records, I had little reason for complaint. They showed that every First Lady in recent history had drawn from staffs of similar size, the average number from 1971 – 76 being 28. Betty Ford had 26; I had 21." Mrs. Carter, during her tenure, used the professional staffs of various federal agencies to assist her in her mental health work. In some cases that worked well. Letitia Baldridge wrote in *Diamonds and Diplomats* that she had about forty people under her on the First Lady's staff during the Kennedy Administration. But such numbering, while it can be used as a political football, is not all that germane — names, numbers, and personnel have often been shifted from one budget to another to distort surveys of staff size.

In 1981, the Reagan Administration was preoccupied with cutting as many federal jobs as possible. This campaign to shrink the size of government was constantly watched by people of all political persuasions. Some thought cuts would dramatically affect direct social service delivery; others thought the cuts were not deep enough. This job-cutting campaign affected the First Lady's staff as well.

Nancy Reagan felt strongly that the East Wing, her staff, should not be exempt from any effort to reduce the size of government and control costs. Throughout my time with her, she remained concerned about limiting the number of her staff and monitoring its expenses. It became an in-house joke that if a staff member were offered a complimentary, upgraded hotel room that would have meant no additional expense, he was to refuse it. As part of an elaborate spoof, Mrs. Reagan once videotaped a goodbye message for a favorite advance man who was known for an occasional extravagance and was now retiring. She read a trumped-up letter from the manager of a major hotel requesting payment for the man's stay in an elegant suite of rooms. "Robert," she said, "I've received a letter from the manager of that hotel in Los Angeles requesting payment for your suite of rooms." Then she added, "He certainly must have meant single room, not a suite!"

Mrs. Reagan was watchful of staff spending but didn't force these restrictions only on us. Having spent many evenings traveling with her, I observed that she always ordered modestly from the usually very expensive room-service menu, regularly choosing the least expensive entree and picking a piece of fruit from the complimentary fruit basket for dessert. In some cities either I or

Experienced army wife, Mamie Eisenhower, who had maintained 29 homes in as many years — from apartments to mansions — checks the White House pantry while Head Butler, Charles Ficklin, prepares the shopping list.

Nancy Reagan meets with her Chief of Staff, and other members of the senior staff frequently. During this meeting, held in the Chief of Staff's office, the anti-drug campaign is discussed.

her secretary would fix her a breakfast of decaffeinated coffee and fruit without even calling room service. Since security requirements dictated that ordering meals and serving was usually left to a staff member, cutting a grapefruit left from the previous day and brewing a cup of Brim were added to my routine. She never complained about my lack of training as a waiter, although one time while I was trying to serve a salad to Mrs. Reagan and her son Ron in her room at the Waldorf-Astoria in New York, I distinctly remember sending lettuce and cabbage flying all over the table.

Nancy Reagan's full-time staff during my tenure (1982-86) usually numbered 18. These individuals were on the First Lady's payroll. In addition, calligraphers and social office person-

nel, paid from the household budget since their responsibilities related directly to household social functions, worked under my general direction. It is important to remember that the White House social office, though it is housed in the east wing and is the First Lady's responsibility, also serves the President by planning and managing all events held in the Rose Garden, on the south lawn, and inside the White House — from briefings, meetings, breakfasts, receptions, and concerts all the way up to state visits. In addition, we also had help from speech writers on the President's staff, and at least one individual from the President's correspondence office was assigned to sort and answer the First Lady's mail which averaged about four thousand pieces a month.

Julie Nixon Eisenhower shows White House visitors the prayer on the mantel written by John Adams: ". . . to Bestow The Best of Blessings on THIS HOUSE and All that shall Inhabit it . . ."

Julia Grant chats with her successor, Lucy Hayes, at the luncheon reception for newly-inaugurated President Rutherford Hayes. Mrs. Grant considered her White House years "the happiest period" of her life. (overleaf)

Mrs. Reagan's staff included a director or chief of staff, press secretary, director of special projects and policy, director of scheduling and advance, social secretary, and an executive assistant for the First Lady. Each of the senior staff members had assistants reporting to them. The First Lady also had a detail, or group, of Secret Service agents assigned specifically to protect her just as the President had.

The First Lady's staff is housed in the wing of the White House built by Franklin Roosevelt during World War II. "East Wing" has become synonymous with the First Lady's staff; but this arm of the White House, attached to the residence by a glass colonnade running parallel to the First Lady's garden, also houses the office of the military attaché to the President, a major portion of the President's legislative staff, and the White House visitors' office. All in all, about one hundred people work there. Betty Ford once remarked that if the West Wing was the mind of the nation, then the East Wing was the heart.

What do all the members of a First Lady's staff do? The staff exists to carry out those duties the First Lady interprets as supporting the President and any and all of her own projects. I never saw our staff used to carry out any personal agenda of Mrs. Reagan, rather we were there to help her to perform her best in her official capacity. In planning and orchestrating official activities Mrs. Reagan and I, as staff director, developed a close working relationship.

The senior staff met together three mornings a week to plan and schedule events (usually six to nine months ahead), to discuss issues facing the First Lady, and to refine events of the day at hand. There was a healthy degree of interaction with the west wing staff based on the President's schedule and other issues which might affect the First Lady. I would call some of these issues substantive, such as the President's drug abuse policy; others were matters of scheduling and travel. For most of my time in the east wing, I attended meetings in the west wing of the President's senior staff led by Jim Baker and, later, Don Regan. The good relationship between the two wings of the White House was unique to the Reagan Administration and it was due in part to Mrs. Reagan's interest in politics and her husband's schedule, as well as to individuals on the President's staff who had a genuine interest in Mrs. Reagan's success as First Lady. This effective communication removed, to a large extent, the labeling in previous administrations of the east wing staff as second rate. The east wing staff was still occasionally described as less capable or more prone to infighting, but I would challenge these characterizations. Everyone on our small staff worked very hard and long hours; and I think everyone felt that we were involved in important work, especially when it came to the antidrug crusade, foreign travel, and political campaigns.

The job of chief of staff has evolved since the days of Isabella Hagner James. In previous administrations the First Ladies' staff directors were also press secretaries or social secretaries as was the case with Mamie Eisenhower's Mary Jane McCaffree, Jackie Kennedy's Tish Baldridge, Lady Bird Johnson's Liz Carpenter, Pat Nixon's Constance Stuart and Helen McCain Smith, and Betty Ford's Sheila Weidenfeld. I was the second man to serve as staff director and when I left we had a good mix of men and women on the staff. As chief of staff, I interpreted my role as that of orchestra leader.

Mrs. Reagan had direct and frequent contact with many members of the staff; and yet I had the ultimate responsibility for making certain everything ran smoothly and for providing her with briefings on issues and options that would allow her to make knowledgeable choices. Each person had a specific job to perform and communication between staff members had to be very frequent. My practice was to either meet with the First Lady or talk with her by telephone early every morning. I reviewed the morning news and the day's schedule and briefed her on details, and we exchanged views on things that

Frances Cleveland enjoys a quiet moment by the window at the end of the second floor corridor, a favorite spot of White House residents. Mrs. Cleveland was the only bride of a president to be married in the mansion.

needed attention that day. Then came the morning staff meeting; its agenda dealt with the schedule for the day and perhaps some larger issue or planning for months ahead. Sometimes a crisis overshadowed our regular work. Sometimes part of our staff moved to a new location for a while — such as when Mrs. Reagan's father was hospitalized and then died in Arizona, or when Queen Elizabeth visited California for ten days in 1983 or when the President entered the Bethesda Naval Hospital for cancer surgery.

I'll never forget my first spring on the job. We had shifted operations and several staff members to Santa Barbara to help produce a country/western concert in the "Young Performers At The White House" series at a ranch high in the Santa Ynez mountains, neighboring the Reagans'. We made it a practice to have staff meetings in the station wagon we used for the daily trek up the mountains from Santa Barbara or on bales of hay on the makeshift stage in the barn. Flexibility was a key. And there was always work to be done.

In the past, press inquiries directed at a First Lady were answered hesitatingly, if at all. In the very early days, women like Dolley Madison answered reporters' questions herself. Julia Gardiner Tyler had her own unique way of handling the press. She hired a press agent who was expected to "sound her praise, near and far." By the 1880s inquiries regarding the First Lady were handled by the President's staff, and in the case of Frances Cleveland, by the President himself. Cleveland so resented press questions about his wife that he referred to the press as "ghouls." Edith Roosevelt directed Isabella Hagner James to handle reporters' questions. Alice Roosevelt sometimes went against her stepmother's strict rules of not allowing the family and press to interact; she not only answered questions herself but approached reporters on her own to give opinions.

Nancy Reagan greets Queen Elizabeth II during the British Monarch's ten-day visit to California in 1983. Mrs. Reagan hosted a dinner for 500 on a sound stage at Twentieth Century-Fox.

As reporters became more and more a prominent fixture in the White House, First Ladies gained confidence in dealing with them. Ellen Wilson granted several interviews during her husband's campaign, but it was Florence Harding who first spoke directly and regularly with the press. Before he became President, Warren Harding had been the owner and editor of a newspaper, *The Marion Star*, and Mrs. Harding worked as its business manager. She was the first First Lady to appreciate the growing professionalism of women journalists. She regularly invited them upstairs to the private quarters where she often discussed political as well as social issues. She demurred, though, about allowing direct quotes. Her immediate successor, Grace Coolidge, was forbidden to grant interviews by her husband; but once when asked to make a public speech, she raised her expressive hands and delivered her remarks in sign language. She had been a teacher of the deaf in her youth. Eleanor Roosevelt, like Mrs. Harding, was comfortable with the press and she instituted weekly press conferences. No First Lady since has chosen to follow Mrs. Roosevelt's example.

Early twentieth-century First Ladies had often used their social secretaries for a variety of roles: schedule coordinator, personal assistant, project liaison. After Eleanor Roosevelt, Bess Truman reverted to this tradition as did Mamie Eisenhower. When Jacqueline Kennedy hired Pamela Turnure to be the first press secretary to a First Lady, that job was permanently established.

Today the job of press secretary is next in importance to the coordinating role of the chief of staff. Experience, the turn of events, and Nancy Reagan herself showed us very quickly that the press secretary must work in the shadow of her boss, have constant and quick access to her, be able to help answer very complicated or controversial questions, and have the confidence of the media. Sheila Tate and, later, Elaine Crispen performed these functions extremely well. Liz Carpenter working for Lady Bird Johnson also stands out as a well liked and an extremely capable press secretary. UPI reporter

Helen Thomas gave Helen McClain Smith, Pat Nixon's secretary, rave reviews, saying that even during the tense days of Watergate, Smith was a particularly honest press secretary.

The White House press corps has grown dramatically and never has a larger contingent of reporters and correspondents been assigned to cover the First Lady than today. We traveled with a regular contingent of between ten and twenty reporters, photographers, and cameramen. We added dozens at cities where we stopped for a speech or special event.

Today the press keeps constant surveillance on the First Lady, and her press secretary must be in touch with her boss many times a day to be able to maintain credibility. When Betty Ford and, later, Rosalynn Carter took secret trips to New York to purchase clothes, they did not even inform their press secretaries who were blindsided when reporters got news of the trips. After that, the First Ladies kept their press secretaries fully informed of all trips or appearances outside the White House.

Although Nancy Reagan had strong political

Some consider Mrs. Reagan's appearance as "Second Hand Rose" at Washington's annual Gridiron Club dinner to be the turning point in her image in the national media.

instincts from the beginning, as time went on she grew more confident in working with the press. Always guarded, she was often accused of unnecessary stiffness and formality, but after the first bumpy year in the White House, her relations with the press steadily improved. Her instinct to control her reactions and hold her personal feelings inside may have caused her trouble initially but later it seems to have contributed to a more positive relationship with reporters. Nancy Reagan has never been one to blurt out a response without considering its consequences.

What turned around Nancy Reagan's initial negative image in the national media? Some political and media analysts point to specific events. They mention the self-deprecating humor she displayed in her "Second Hand Rose" performance at Washington's annual Gridiron Club dinner or her speech at the Alf Landon

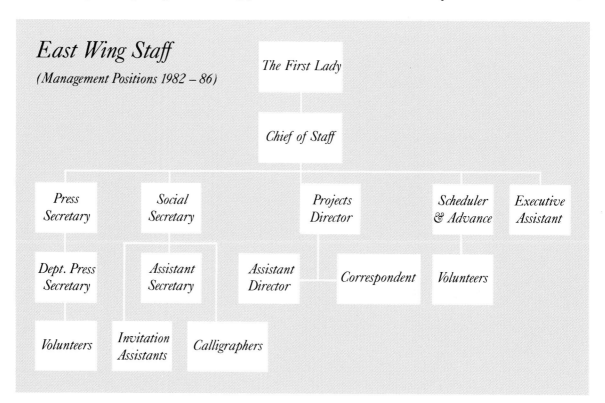

dinner in New York, when, standing in for the President, she poked fun at her Queen Nancy image, saying, "Oh, I'd never wear a crown. . .it would mess up my hair." But in my opinion, her change of image was due to sustained exposure to the media during her campaign to increase public awareness of the national crisis of drug and alcohol abuse. As they became better acquainted with her, observed her at close range in all conditions, writers and television correspondents began to see that the person they had characterized as a plastic fashion plate actually had a large heart, caring feelings, a good sense of humor, and a rather appealing degree of vulnerability. Some in the media still maintain her improved image was a public relations ploy, but Nancy Reagan insisted she never wanted to be anyone but herself. Time and time again when asked what she would advise future First Ladies, she answered with a resounding, "Be yourself. Don't try to fill a mold created by someone else."

I'll never forget the night in the winter of 1982 when she visited STRAIGHT, INC., a drug rehabilitation center in Orlando, Florida. After listening for three solid hours to young boys and girls tell about how they had prostituted themselves for drugs, burned crosses in their arms, taken insecticides, turned their younger siblings and pets on to drugs, and every other imaginable horror related to drugs, Mrs. Reagan was asked to talk to the group of about three hundred. With no prepared speech and puffy eyes, red from crying, she turned to the parents first and told them how she knew no hurt could be as painful as the hurt between parent and child and that she admired them for acknowledging their family problems and for getting help. Next, fighting back more tears, she turned to the children and told them she loved them, that she wanted them to fight hard to be drug free, and that the world needed them. By the end we were all crying, even the Secret Service. It was hard to see how this kind of raw feeling or caring could have been fabricated; and the writers and correspondents present began to see another side to this woman who likes to wear red.

Shortly after this trip she attended the international convention of PRIDE (Parents' Resources In Drug Education). After speaking to the young people in the audience, they hoisted her on their shoulders spontaneously and carried her around the convention hall, hero style. As her earrings went flying across the room, reporters may have wondered what these young people were finding in Nancy Reagan that they hadn't.

Other First Ladies have also had their bouts with strained public relations as well as problems of public perception. In the campaign of 1828 Rachel Jackson, the wife of candidate Andrew Jackson, was the target of a vile mud-slinging attack. Broken in spirit, she had no interest in serving as First Lady; she became ill and died before she had to fulfill the role she dreaded so much. Northern papers called Mary Todd Lincoln a "southern sympathizer" and the southern papers called her a traitor to her "Kentucky heritage." After several years of constant public

Eleanor Roosevelt poses as Whistler's Mother in a skit at the Gridiron Widows' buffet she held for women journalists and cabinet wives in protest against the Gridiron Club's male-only policy.

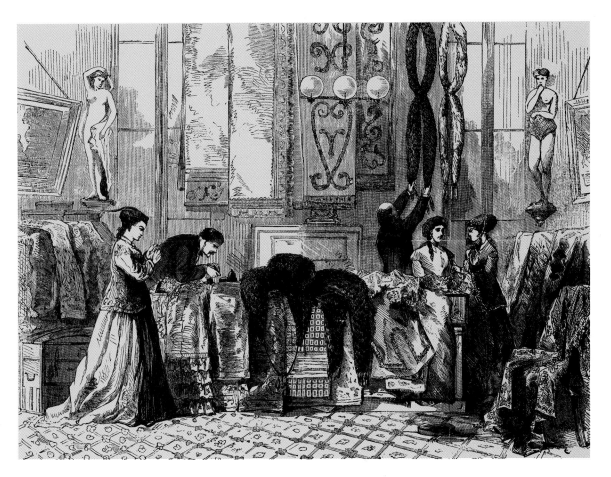

Viewers examine Mary Lincoln's elaborate gowns and furs when, after her husband's assassination, they were put on display in New York. She was accused of unpatriotic extravagance during the Civil War.

criticism, a hardened Mrs. Lincoln wrote "I know full well by experience power and high position do not ensure a bed of roses."

Even lovely Frances Cleveland met harsh criticism when she ordered the gates of the White House grounds closed because rude tourists walking about the gardens picked up her toddlers and kissed them while a helpless nurse stood by. Lucy Hayes's ban on liquor made her the butt of jokes from the "wet" press, and her famous nickname "Lemonade Lucy" survives in White House lore. Eleanor Roosevelt's active role initially met with negative editorials. Then Bess Truman's inactivity was unpopular with the press who had come to appreciate Mrs. Roosevelt. Betty Ford's frank answers to "60 Minutes" interviewer Morley Safer's questions on premarital sex prompted picketers in front of the White House.

When the American people elect a President, they get two people for the price of one. In the future, legislation may provide the First Lady with some financial compensation for the work required of her. A forerunner of this movement may have been the recent, only partially successful, effort by State Department wives to receive compensation for the full-time duties of an ambassador's spouse. To meet the heavy responsibilities thrust upon most cabinet-level officials, their spouses must also provide almost full-time support. Some will say that no couple is forced to choose such a career; but the government needs capable, accomplished individuals willing to serve the country. It may be time to acknowledge the fact that most official jobs require hard-working spouses. Most government officials would find it difficult to perform without one.

In the case of the presidency certain jobs must be done by a wife or a surrogate. I would divide the responsibilities of any First Lady into two categories: "required" and "optional, but highly desirable." The first list is longer. It would include overseeing the appearance of the state rooms, grounds, and private family quarters of the White House; setting a tone for the nearly one million visitors who come to the mansion as guests or on public tours each year; planning and supervising all facets of White House entertaining — everything from flower arrangements to lighting to selection of performers; acting as hostess for presidential receptions, briefings, meetings, and meals held within the White House; acting as hostess at receptions and meetings held in the name of First Lady; acting as sponsor of hundreds of national and international charity and public-interest events; overseeing correspondence; traveling with the President as required; some degree of involvement in political campaigns; overseeing the domestic and official staff; keeping some semblance of harmony and communication among children, family and friends; maintaining her own grooming and wardrobe.

In the optional, but highly desirable category, I would place frequent availability to the press; independent travel as a goodwill ambassador in support of the President's goals; adopting and working for one or more social causes; acting as an unofficial advisor to the President and making some substantial improvement in the White House.

Few First Ladies in recent history have had time to sit for hours by the fireside. A day in the White House is a long one. There is little historical data on the nocturnal habits of previous occupants, but I know that Mrs. Reagan requires very little sleep. By her own admission she is a constant "worrier." By any account she puts in a very long day. Here is what one might look like:

6:30 a.m.
Breakfast, newspapers, morning news shows. Mrs. Reagan rises early. When traveling, the morning wake-up call usually finds her already awake and watching television. She is an inveterate channel switcher at news time and she reads four or five different newspapers a day. She eats a light breakfast.

8:30 a.m.
Exercise. Mrs. Reagan is committed to regular

exercise as is the President. Exercise equipment is installed in one of the rooms in the family quarters.

9:00 a.m.
Dressed. Telephone briefings with the staff.

9:30 a.m.
Meeting with her executive assistant to review mail, write letters, answer requests, return edited drafts of speeches, and more.

10:00 a.m.
Meet with chief usher, White House chef, and florist. Review arrangements for upcoming events, make menu selections, and schedule tastings.

10:30 a.m.
Make a phone call to a mother who has written and is distressed about her son's involvement in drugs.

10:45 a.m.
Hair combed in White House beauty salon.

11:00 a.m.
Coffee with the wife of a visiting foreign dignitary. One-on-one or in a small group, the ladies usually share stories about their own countries and information on their special concerns. Meetings like this help reinforce U.S. foreign policy goals in a general way and increase communication and friendship between the countries.

12:00 p.m.
Prepare for luncheon speech.

12:30 p.m.
Address National Advertising Council, or similar group, at a local hotel, receive award for work in drug abuse, eat lunch.

2:00 p.m.
Return to White House. Return telephone calls.

2:30 p.m.
Staff meeting. Approximately once a week,

the First Lady meets with her staff in a lengthy planning session. She receives reports on the status of her special projects and decides what to do about them.

4:45 p.m.
Greet in the Oval Office the Easter Seal child or another special group that has come to see the President.

5:15 p.m.
Attend a reception with the President in the East Room to honor a special group.

6:30 p.m.
Watch evening news with the President while eating dinner on TV trays.

8:30 p.m.
Brief scheduled stop at a nearby benefit dinner to receive an award from a voluntary drug group for her crusade. Another speech.

9:15 p.m.
Return home.

11:00 p.m.
Retire. Read in bed.

All these activities may not take place in one day, but they could. Many days the schedule is even more crowded, although a good staff prepares a schedule that allows time to accomplish everything while providing time for the family. Despite very crowded schedules, I never heard Nancy Reagan say, "You have planned too much for me, slow down." She was always hard working and usually a mile ahead of her staff. When she asked you a question she almost always already knew the answer. The primary requirement for any advance man who works for Mrs. Reagan is that his legs be long enough and his energy level high enough to walk faster than she does. She is usually a full pace ahead of everyone else.

In one of her rare statements to the press, Bess Truman answered the question of what is most necessary for being First Lady. "Good health and a sense of humor" was sturdy Bess's

comment. There is much truth to that. Health has often restricted a First Lady's activities. High blood pressure, in fact, may have been a factor in limiting Bess Truman's public appearances. Mamie Eisenhower suffered from a weak heart, and often had to rest in bed during the day to have strength for official dinners at night. This curtailed her public appearances outside of the White House. Jacqueline Kennedy's pregnancy removed her from all social events in the spring and summer of 1963; so her sister-in-law Eunice Shriver substituted on at least one occasion. When cancer surgery eclipsed Betty Ford's activities in the fall of 1974, her daughter, Susan, served as surrogate First Lady at a state dinner.

The physical and mental strain of the job which Mrs. Reagan once described as being "more than just full-time, it's overtime" bears heavily on even the most enthusiastic First Ladies. Personal and official duties make the job one that many women — or men — would find almost impossible.

Although they were often thought of as formal, the Reagans enjoy nothing more than their informal TV-tray dinners together in the President's study, while they watch the evening news.

The Diplomat at Home & Abroad

The weather reports that morning were threatening. The military attaché to the American ambassador kept in constant touch with weather stations in Normandy to determine whether Nancy Reagan would be able to fly by helicopter, as planned, to the U.S. cemetery at Omaha Beach. Paris was warm and overcast with good visibility but Normandy was experiencing a typical fog roll-in. The alternate plan was to take a small U.S. military plane to an airport near the cemetery and go the balance of the way in a motorcade. With the winding roads in Normandy, this could have meant a serious delay in the arrival time which could have inconvenienced the officials and the crowds waiting for her to lead the somber ceremony.

Although the weather in Normandy was still not clear at the scheduled departure time, we decided to chance the helicopter trip. Mrs. Reagan was a bit restless as she reviewed her speech on the two-hour trip from Paris. Then the chopper landed on its white target and Nancy Reagan stepped out, accompanied by military attachés carrying black umbrellas to keep the First Lady dry. Intermittent light rain added to the drama of a thousand white crosses stretching across the beachhead high above the Atlantic as the First Lady, representing the President, joined representatives of several foreign countries at a ceremony commemorating the thirty-eighth anniversary of the allied invasion. It was a moving solo diplomatic mission for the First Lady. A low, sad military march sounded as Mrs. Reagan walked to the grave of the only woman buried at Omaha Beach. The First Lady's speech was brief, but she felt both the history of what had gone before and the history of the moment, and she had to stop several times during her remarks to choke back tears.

Later she exchanged flags with a French woman whose father had built the invasion museum at Arromanches — a tribute to American

*R*epresenting the president at ceremonies commemorating the 38th anniversary of the landing at Omaha Beach in Normandy during World War II, Mrs. Reagan pays homage to those buried there.

fighting men. We lunched at the house of a French family overlooking the English Channel. On that day, June 6, 1982, I think Nancy Reagan began to see what she could accomplish on her own in extending the goodwill of the American people to people of other countries. She undertook other diplomatic missions, both alone and with the President, but the powerful image of that day in Normandy will remain with me, and I think, with her, for a very long time.

Diplomatic missions and involvement in international issues by First Ladies are not unique to Nancy Reagan. Throughout our country's history, First Ladies have provided a variety of goodwill and diplomatic initiatives. Martha Washington was an important symbol for the women of Revolutionary America. While imports from England were boycotted, she made sacrifices of food and services so that they would be available for soldiers. She also established, in each of the Colonies, a network of women's groups that pooled finances and much-needed clothing for the Continental Army.

Dolley Madison was a symbol of endurance

*M*ilitary attaches attempt to keep Mrs. Reagan dry during the ceremonies in remembrance of the Allied invasion. This is the day she began to see what good a First Lady could accomplish on diplomatic missions.

*E*dith and Woodrow Wilson partake of Christmas dinner at the front during their trip to Europe after World War I. At the treaty signing at Versailles no women were invited, but she observed from behind the draperies.

and strength when she refused to leave the burning capital during the War of 1812, despite threats that she would be taken hostage. In the face of attempts to move the capital back to Philadelphia, she encouraged the rebuilding of a charred Washington and the permanent establishment of the city as our nation's capital.

During the Mexican-American War, Sarah Polk was quick to promote solutions to the conflict. During the Civil War, Mary Todd Lincoln made unannounced trips to hospitals to visit the wounded as well as going to the front lines to bolster morale. On these trips she often made her views on the war known to those she encountered at the front. Although she was well intentioned, more than once the President had to put Mrs. Lincoln's involvement in war matters in proper perspective.

During World War I, Edith Wilson's sewing machine hummed through long days and nights sewing wool pajamas and socks for the Red Cross to aid in the war effort. She also helped sell war bonds and was involved in decoding long messages from foreign leaders to her husband. Thus she was aware of many military maneuvers and details of the peace talks. She was rewarded with

a trip to Paris when her husband went to sign the peace treaty, and while there she was present at most State Department briefings. Henry White, a well-traveled American diplomat, called her a "valuable channel for communication." He was also impressed with her "right headedness" in the complicated issues of the treaty. During the actual negotiations, she was called in to stop a presidential assistant from speaking prematurely to the press and she deferred the controversy to Secretary of State Robert Lansing.

At the official treaty signing ceremony at Versailles Palace, no women were invited to attend, but Edith used her wily ways to get Clemenceau to admit her to the Hall of Mirrors so that she could observe the signing. Her place of honor was behind heavy red-brocade draperies in a small alcove. Later she described herself as an unsuspected listener, "happy, but hot."

There was no attempt to hide Florence Harding at the Conference on the Limitation of Armaments held in Washington in 1921. Each day she went to the meetings and sat in the viewing box with the wives of foreign leaders whom she had invited. Mrs. Harding openly boasted of her knowledge of and keen interest in national politics. She was credited with steering her husband toward a more conservative approach to foreign policy.

Few First Ladies promoted international understanding more openly than did Eleanor Roosevelt. During World War I, she said that she wanted to do all she could to prevent future wars and she often wrote that she felt frustrated that the peace movement made such limited progress. She delivered the keynote address for the 1937 No-Foreign-War Crusade and in 1938 spoke at the then annual conference on the Cause and Cure of War. She wrote at that time, "If we are going to have peace in this world, we will have to find the machinery to draw us together and make

During World War II, Eleanor Roosevelt did all she could to further the effort. She boosted morale by visiting servicemen at home and abroad, and was assistant chief of the Office of Civilian Defense.

us function together." During World War II, as First Lady, she wrote that she could identify with all American women who were going through "the same slow death." After the war, when she was no longer First Lady, she was rewarded for her efforts for peace by an appointment as a U.S. delegate to the United Nations and she served as chairman of the U.N. Commission on Human Rights. In this capacity she helped draft "A Plan To Preserve World Peace," for which she was nominated for the American Peace Award.

During her long tenure as First Lady, Mrs. Roosevelt traveled to the South Pacific and to Europe as well. One young State Department official remembers encountering her in London shortly after the war during a time of critical shortages of power. Mrs. Roosevelt was climbing the many flights of stairs to her meeting at the U.S. mission headquarters. The young woman asked if she could call an elevator to take the former First Lady upstairs. With a firm rebuke Mrs. Roosevelt assured her that the stairs would be just fine and reminded her that all visitors had been asked to save electricity in every way possible.

Eleanor Roosevelt's interpretation of her role was unique in many ways. She was especially well prepared for diplomacy by her schooling and travel abroad as a young girl. She made many trips alone to places where, because of his physical disability, the President could not go. Few other First Ladies have had the background, inclination, or opportunity to create a position the way Mrs. Roosevelt did.

Most First Ladies have had a more subtle impact on their husband's foreign policy and on foreign leaders themselves. When the War of 1812 ended, Dolley Madison celebrated not in the White House, which had been burned by the British, but in Octagon House a few blocks away. As her husband signed the long-awaited treaty she flung open the doors of this temporary

Some 40 years after Edith Wilson had to hide behind the draperies at Versailles to observe the World War I peace treaty, Jacqueline Kennedy sits beside Charles DeGaulle at a sumptuous state dinner there. (overleaf)

The Diplomat at Home & Abroad

51

executive mansion to the public. "Peace! Peace!" she shouted of the crowds awaiting news. In this way, Mrs. Madison set a tone of renewed patriotism throughout the nation as well as in the burned city, as it began the arduous task of rebuilding.

Many presidential wives have provided a calming measure of confidence for their husbands during critical negotiations. This was true of Mrs. Andrew Johnson who ultimately affected her husband's policy toward the South. Her gentle nature is described by some as promoting his interest in peace and humanitarian efforts. Lucy Webb Hayes, in similar fashion, influenced her husband's Reconstruction policies. As a result the tone of his policies was more cooperative and conciliatory rather than coercive. One who questioned the Hayes policy on Reconstruction came away from a session with the First Lady saying, "She is shrewd and up on current events."

Ida McKinley had a rather odd approach to promoting peace. During the Spanish-American War she proposed a peace plan based on converting everyone to Methodism.

Mrs. McKinley's successor Edith Roosevelt was wiser and more discreet. During the Russo-Japanese War she served as a secret emissary between her husband and British envoy Cecil Spring-Rice. Spring-Rice was an old Roosevelt family friend and Edith had great rapport with him, but the President's direct communiques caused problems for the senior British envoy, Mortimer Durand. Roosevelt wanted Spring-Rice's observations and counsel so a plan was devised aimed to avoid disturbing regular diplomatic channels. Spring-Rice's messages were coded for the First Lady only, then she passed them along for the President's use.

I would characterize Nancy Reagan's contribution to American diplomacy as subtle but meaningful. She has entertained more foreign heads of state than any other First Lady in history. Her easy charm and attractiveness draws heads of state and other diplomats to her side during receptions, meetings, and dinners. They give her own brand of entertaining high marks.

The Reagans have continued a tradition begun in the Eisenhower Administration of entertaining the entire Washington diplomatic corps once a year. These events have evolved from formal receptions to concerts to barbecues.

I'll never forget one afternoon when Nancy Reagan entertained the Washington diplomatic corps on the south lawn. The temperature had reached 100 degrees and the humidity stood at 95 percent. Since it was the Boston Pops' one hundredth anniversary, she had asked them to play a concert on the south portico of the White House. How could we know, when planning six months before, that the reception would fall on the day of the President's first cancer surgery? I suggested canceling the affair, but Mrs. Reagan insisted that by going ahead with the schedule she could share the President's feeling of confidence and "business as usual." Not only did she speak on behalf of the President that afternoon but she stood in a receiving line to greet nearly three hundred representatives of foreign countries. She told me afterwards that the supportive comments of the diplomats and their wives about the President's health had actually strengthened her that afternoon. For an official in Washington it might be all too easy to shrug off the occasion as insignificant; but to the chiefs of foreign missions, it showed that a President's wife could represent a strong government not weakened by the President's ill health. I am sure that many ambassadors cabled back to their capitals a message of reassurance from Washington.

Twice during my tenure Mrs. Reagan hosted the same kind of diplomatic reception in New York at the time of the annual meeting of the U.N. General Assembly. Hosting an affair away from the White House always posed difficult security and logistical problems; but between the east wing staff and the White House advance office, we were usually able to plan events that were both gracious and newsworthy. Such was

P ressed to leave the White House before the invading British arrived, Dolley Madison packed a trunk full of important papers and cut the portrait of George Washington from its frame to save it from destruction.

*B*achelor President Buchanan and the Prince of Wales honor George Washington at his tomb at Mount Vernon. *Harriet Lane, the President's niece (here holding a parasol), served as her uncle's hostess.*

the case when Soviet Foreign Minister Andrei Gromyko accepted the President's invitation to meet during one of these New York diplomatic receptions and the following year when Nicaraguan president Daniel Ortega attended with his wife and spoke with the President.

Another diplomatic event took place away from the White House during the 1983 economic summit in Williamsburg, Virginia. Mrs. Reagan transformed the garden at the historic Governors' Mansion into a tented setting for dinner, and as the hostess and the only first lady present, she moved among the heads of state to make them feel at home.

The Reagans' entertaining during state visits has been a partnership. While the President certainly never involved himself in selecting

flowers for the tables and Mrs. Reagan never poured over briefing papers from the State Department, their easy confidence and nonverbal communication put their guests at ease. Even those who came to Washington with affairs of grave concern and points of view significantly different from the President's went away, I believe, convinced of the sincerity and desire for goodwill on the part of the President and First Lady.

The First Lady's preparation for state dinners always begins months in advance and includes short written briefings on the country, its political system, and of course, its leaders and first lady. From the selection of after-dinner entertainment to the guests' seating arrangement, Mrs. Reagan manages the details. This

*O*ne high note of the whirlwind tour of Europe in *1985 was Mrs. Reagan's official meeting with the Pope in the Vatican. Their acquaintanceship was renewed during his visit to the United States in September 1987.*

care contributes to a more harmonious environment for the substantive business to be undertaken. Mrs. Reagan is always on the lookout for entertainers for state dinners. She tries to plan a wide range of entertainment and, if at all possible, one that features favorites of the visiting head of state.

The entertainment portion of the dinner always requires rehearsals and sound checks and, for dance groups and chamber orchestras, special staging. Usually the entertainment went off without a hitch.

The only major problem I can recall occurred when the Reagans asked Tommy Tune and Twiggy to bring a portion of their successful musical *Singing in the Rain* to the East Room. Several months prior to the actual date, I traveled to New York, met with the artists, and completed negotiations for them to come to the White House. When we called to confirm rehearsal

time, the stars were away on another engagement and were surprised to learn that their manager had never telephoned to cancel the White House appearance. The shock was all mine. We had only forty-eight hours to book new entertainment. Karen Akers, a superb performer, stepped in to fill the bill, and the First Lady's staff had learned a valuable lesson of always checking and double-checking commitments from performers.

Mrs. Reagan sharpened her diplomatic skills at many events with foreign emissaries in Washington. For example, during a luncheon reception with Foreign Minister Gromyko, he whispered to her to tell the President, "We seek peace," to which she replied, also in a whisper, that Gromyko should remind *himself* that Americans seek peace every day.

Mrs. Reagan frequently had opportunities to meet with first ladies from other nations who were accompanying their husbands on state visits or unofficial visits or were traveling alone. Mrs. Reagan took this opportunity beyond its teatime

character by organizing a first-time-ever worldwide conference of first ladies. In April 1985 seventeen first ladies joined Nancy Reagan in the East Room of the White House to talk seriously about the approaching peril of drug and alcohol abuse. First ladies from every continent were invited. The guest list was made up from countries with whom the United States has diplomatic relations. As expected, some of the countries with the most serious interest in the subject sent their first ladies to attend. While several first ladies denied that their own people were actually threatened or that this was a serious problem in their countries, after two days all of them went away better educated on the issue and perhaps more willing, if only privately, to admit that the problem exists in *every* nation around the world.

After day-long briefings at the White House the first ladies flew to Atlanta aboard an Air Force plane to attend a meeting of PRIDE, an international group of parents and children organized to fight drug abuse. I'll never forget the moment when all of the first ladies were called on stage to be recognized by the young leaders of the conference. This experience, we found out later from several of them, had direct bearing on increasing their own public involvement in the fight to curb this epidemic.

Did this conference have any diplomatic value? Judging from the cables sent to Mrs. Reagan after the conference and the educational processes started by these women in their own countries, the meeting had immediate good results. The diplomatic value of such a venture — improved bilateral and multilateral relations between the United States and its allies — is harder to evaluate. What each first lady communicated to the head of state when she returned home we can only surmise, but based on our own political process, her report must have reflected goodwill for our nation.

Jacqueline Kennedy, with her sister Lee Radziwill, travelled to India in 1962. Photo coverage of her in various exotic settings like this, captured public fancy and helped make her an international figure.

In fact, this meeting was judged to be such a success that Mrs. Reagan invited a different group of first ladies to attend a similar conference at the United Nations during its fortieth anniversary celebration. On this occasion, Nancy Reagan became the first American First Lady to speak at the UN during her official tenure. Eighteen first ladies attended and heard devastating stories told by young people themselves of how drug abuse can destroy lives. By the end of the conference there were calls to meet again, to bring the first ladies of many countries together to address other critical social problems that affect our increasingly smaller world.

When Edith Roosevelt joined her husband, the President, on an official trip to Panama to inspect the digging of the Panama Canal, she became the first First Lady to travel outside of the continental United States. Edith Wilson was the second First Lady to journey abroad when she made her eventful trip with her husband to the Paris peace talks. Bess Truman traveled with her husband to South America by ship. Mamie Eisenhower, an Army wife, had gone around the world with her husband on military assignments. By the time she became First Lady, Mamie preferred to stay at home — more because of her poor health than a lack of interest. She sent her daughter-in-law, Barbara, as an acting First Lady with the President on several trips. The junior Mrs. Eisenhower met with Pope John at the Vatican and toured the Taj Mahal in India.

One reason Bess Truman and Mamie Eisenhower did not go abroad as much as Eleanor Roosevelt was that the two ladies disliked flying. Mrs. Truman thought flying undignified, and enjoyed the style of train travel. Mamie Eisenhower suffered from Ménière's disease, which affected the inner ear and restricted her flying. Jacqueline Kennedy was a jet setter in more ways than one — she loved flying. This accounts in part for her eagerness to travel to Europe and the Middle East with and without the President. Air Force planes, by 1961, were regularly at the disposal of presidential families, and the Kennedys took full advantage of this. As presidential travel abroad escalated, chief executives were often accompanied by their First Ladies.

In 1961 Jacqueline Kennedy travelled with her husband to France and Austria. In France she beguiled President Charles de Gaulle and in Austria she charmed Russian Premier Nikita Khrushchev. In Vienna, Mrs. Kennedy participated in an impressive Mass at the Cathedral of St. John that was said "for peace between the peoples of the world."

Pat Nixon traveled with her husband to the Soviet Union and to China. Her sightseeing in China was shared with an enthusiastic audience of millions of television viewers back home. Mrs. Nixon became the second First Lady to make official solo trips on behalf of the President. She was well received in West Africa. In Ghana, a tribal chief gave her an unusual accolade: her visit had created a bond with the United States that "not even a lion could destroy." When she went to Peru immediately following the 1970 earthquake,

a high ranking Peruvian official noted, "Her coming here meant more than anything else President Nixon could have done." *La Prensa*, a Lima newspaper, editorialized, "She has gone beyond the norms of international courtesy and endured fatigue in an example of solidarity."

Rosalynn Carter worked hard during the Camp David peace talks and drafted a call for prayer from all people to help support the success of the talks. Her trip to Latin America as a representative of the President, however, met with controversy. Apparently these national leaders wanted to deal directly with the President of the United States on matters of policy — not his wife. Perhaps this was due in part to cultural differences; but whatever its cause, it led Nancy Reagan to be more modest and cautious in assuming representational responsibilities. Time and time again, from that rainy day in Normandy to her visit to earthquake-torn Mexico

*D*uring her second trip to China, Betty Ford visited a ballet school and was asked to join in a dance. This kind of cultural interchange was hailed as having "done more to cement relations . . . than all the talk of diplomats."

to her meeting with the Pope, she refused to be considered a presidential representative or an official envoy of the United States government. She preferred to represent herself and the American people.

By the time I joined her staff, Mrs. Reagan had already traveled to Canada with the President and attended the 1981 wedding of Prince Charles and Lady Diana. The wedding trip came smack in the middle of controversy over her image at home. The relentless pace of social obligations related to the wedding and the preoccupation of the British with the pomp of the ceremony did not give her an opportunity to practice much substantive diplomacy. The glamour of the wedding trip did little to help her failing image; her meeting in London with artists of the Dance Theatre of Harlem and visit to the Spastic Hospital were quickly overshadowed by wedding mania.

During her first five years in the White House, Nancy Reagan traveled abroad twelve times, and on four of these trips she traveled by herself — to London, Monaco, Rome and Mexico. Prior to each trip she restated her goals of extending American friendship to the people of a foreign country; learning about the country's culture, art, and history; sharing common social concerns with other first ladies; spreading the word about drug abuse; and accompanying the President at official occasions.

To help achieve these objectives, before every trip, I traveled to each country two or three times as Mrs. Reagan's eyes and ears. I returned with options for her schedule. The first demand when planning a foreign trip was to block out the time required for official duties with the President. This meant that on most advance trips we worked very closely with the President's staff. The second requirement was to determine the

In Madrid in May 1985, Nancy Reagan takes a turn at dancing the flamenco. As a measure of worldwide interest in the activities of an American First Lady, this photo appeared in newspapers around the world.

The gardens created by Monet in Giverny, France, was one stop on a densely-packed European trip in 1982. Here Nancy Reagan walks with Gerald van der Kemp, former Inspector General of France's National Museums.

level of involvement in Mrs. Reagan's schedule the hosting first lady would have. Would she be holding a luncheon? Were there special events or causes she wanted to share with our first lady?

Although the Reagans had gone to Canada in 1981 and to the Caribbean in April 1982, the first foreign trip of any length came in June of 1982. This European trip was a whirlwind. In addition to attending the economic summit in France, the President was to visit Germany, Italy, the Vatican, and Great Britain. Planning took months, the trip ten days. Urged on by Mrs. Reagan, I was always on the lookout for drug abuse programs abroad that she could visit. Lacking those, Mrs. Reagan usually chose to visit places where she could talk with children. On our first foray together in France she visited a music school for the blind, met with the families of American victims of terrorist attacks, opened an exhibition of American Impressionists and held a reception for Americans at the Petit Palais, visited Monet's home Giverny, and attended the Paris opera. In addition, Madame Mitterrand gave a luncheon for Mrs. Reagan at the Elysée.

As fast paced and as fascinating as these trips were, they were also filled with ordinary events. I remember one night in Paris when Mrs. Reagan was hungry after an evening event. There was a new McDonald's on the Champs Elysées so I offered to run out for a hamburger. With our advance man sitting in the car, I ran through the golden arches only to find a long line of customers. I couldn't very well announce that I had come for a Big Mac for the First Lady of the United States. Even if my French had been excellent I'm sure I would have been whisked off by the gendarmes on the street corner. When I finally got to the head of the line I congratulated myself for being able to say "well done" in French but promptly forgot how to say "catsup." After a few false starts I was on my way back to the embassy only to find that Mrs. Reagan had found a piece of toast in the ambassador's kitchen and had retired for the night.

Following a magnificent seven-nation economic summit dinner at Versailles we flew to Rome. During the morning rush hour, we raced through the city's crowded streets with Ruth

Rabb, the wife of the American ambassador, to visit a drug program Mrs. Rabb helped found. There Mrs. Reagan heard stories indicating that Italian youths faced the same drug problems confronting young people elsewhere. Following the visit to the drug program, there was an official luncheon at the Quirinal palace and an official audience with the Pope in the Vatican. This provided another human footnote to travel in a presidential entourage.

Vatican protocol dictates that for a formal audience with the Pope, women dress completely in black, long skirts and veils. This necessitated a change of clothes from the outfit the First Lady wore to visit the drug center; and the change was planned down to the split second. Then came the glitch. During the change into black Mrs. Reagan noticed the shoes and dress for her change back to street clothes were missing; they had been inadvertently left on the *Air Force One*. Radio relays back and forth to the airport finally produced a speedy Italian driver

*P*resident and Mrs. Carter escort Pope John Paul II through the White House during his visit to the United States in 1979. One of the largest crowds ever assembled on the White House lawn came to greet him.

The First Lady's Missions Abroad 1981 – 1985

March 1981
State visit to Canada

July 1981
Royal wedding in London*

April 1982
State visits to Jamaica and Barbados

June 1982
Economic summit in France, followed by visits to the Vatican, Italy, Germany, and the United Kingdom

September 1982
Princess Grace's funeral in Monaco*

November 1983
State visits to Japan and Korea

April 1984
Visit to China

June 1984
Economic summit in London; state visit to Ireland; D-Day celebration in Normandy, France

March 1985
Official visit to Quebec City, Canada

May 1985
Economic summit in Germany; visit to Rome*; state visits to Spain and Portugal

August 1985
Earthquake assistance to Mexico City, Mexico*

November 1985
Gorbachev-Reagan summit in Geneva, Switzerland

indicates solo travel

*M*rs. Reagan's two "adopted" Korean children with heart defects get hugs from the First Lady. Scheduled to come to the United States for surgery, they flew on Air Force One with the Reagans in November 1983.

who, within a hairbreadth of the necessary time, arrived with the right clothes. Otherwise Nancy Reagan would have appeared at her next appointment in something like a nun's habit.

On that 1982 diplomatic journey, the First Lady included the dedication of a new wing of a hospital in London and a visit to Phoenix House of Germany, a drug rehabilitation center located on an old farm not far from Bonn. All in all, the trip was exhausting but rewarding. According to the *Baltimore Sun*, on that trip, Nancy Reagan earned the title of "America's best diplomat." In the years that followed, the thirty-sixth First Wife worked hard to keep that title.

Next came an unexpected solo trip to Monaco on September 17, 1982, to attend the funeral of Princess Grace. Mrs. Reagan characterized her trip as one of friendship rather than as a government representative, although she headed the American delegation which included the governor of Pennsylvania, Dick Thornburgh, and the secretary of the Navy, John Lehman, a cousin of Princess Grace. In Monaco Mrs. Reagan was provided with a splendid room at the palace; but we never did figure out how to turn on the water in the sunken tub in the bathroom. On the unusually hot day of the funeral, trying to bring comfort to the mourning family, Mrs. Reagan did not find the job of First Lady particularly easy. This trip came exactly one month after the death of Mrs. Reagan's father and

exactly one month before she would attend the funeral of Bess Truman. For a while there it seemed as if we were in the funeral attending business.

Next on the international schedule was a trip to Japan and Korea, November 8 – 14, 1983 with the President. In Korea Mrs. Reagan visited Boys Town and later "adopted" two Korean children. Both children had come to Mrs. Reagan's attention through an American woman who was working tirelessly to send Korean children with heart defects to the United States for surgery. Shy at first, both children became fast friends with the First Lady and charmed all the passengers on *Air Force One* on the return trip home.

In Japan Mrs. Reagan visited the No drama theatre, stopped to see the oldest Living Legend (a title bestowed on nationally treasured artists) and visited a Japanese school that had been adopted by an American school on Long Island.

Then came the extensive trip to China in April 1984. While in Beijing Nancy Reagan visited a typical commune, had tea with a local family, watched acupuncture at a clinic, and visited tourist attractions such as the Forbidden City, Summer Palace, and the Temple of Heaven. She also stopped at the Beijing zoo to give the thousands of pennies that American school children had collected for the World Wildlife Foundation's "Pennies for Pandas" campaign to help save starving pandas.

The degree of friendship Nancy Reagan met in Deng Xiaoping came as a great surprise. He chatted easily with her and invited her to return to China alone so that he could really "entertain her." Later in the visit she charmed her hosts by wearing a Chinese-style dress that the vice-premier had given her the previous day.

Next came the London economic summit of June 1984 and a sentimental trip to Ireland. The highlight of Mrs. Reagan's stay in Ireland was the

*T*he Temple of Heaven in Beijing was only one of the highlights of Mrs. Reagan's visit to China in April 1984. A surprise was the degree of friendship expressed by Deng Xiaoping.

dedication of the Loyal Davis Chair of Neurosurgery at the College of Neurosurgeons in Dublin. When the president of the college lifted the curtain on a photographic portrait of her father to be hung in a hall of the college, it brought back a flood of memories and tears; but she managed to make a speech and accept an award. This trip was also sentimental for the President because it included a visit to the Reagan ancestral home.

London, oddly enough, was always the most difficult city in which to arrange for Mrs. Reagan to visit social institutions or to meet with children. Everything had to be cleared by Buckingham Palace; and there was a certain reluctance to have a foreign visitor underscore national problems such as drugs. On this trip we finally scheduled a trip to the London zoo and Mrs. Reagan took two classes from a local school with her on a rented bright red double-decker bus.

In the winter of 1985, the Reagans made an official visit to Quebec City. It was bitter cold and security so tight that we couldn't leave the perimeter of the old city. Within its walls we

*H*undreds of terra cotta soldiers stand guard in the ancient tomb in the Chinese city of Xian. As a part of their visit to China in 1984, the Reagans viewed an open air market, an experiment in capitalism.

found a charming old convent school where Mrs. Reagan could visit with the girls and employ her schoolbook French.

In June 1985, we returned to Bonn, Germany, for an economic summit. Since Mrs. Reagan had expressed a desire to talk with the Pope about his concern for children and drug abuse, we were dispatched to meet with Vatican officials. Although this would be a first — no other First Lady had met with the Pope on an issue of this seriousness — the Pope was eager to invite Mrs. Reagan to a meeting. While she was in Rome as the guest of U.S. Ambassador Max Rabb, Mrs. Reagan visited a drug center on the outskirts of Rome with Anna Craxi, wife of the Italian prime minister. President Sandro Pertini, a man affectionately called the "Grandfather of Italy," gave a very small private luncheon for her. This luncheon together with her meeting with the Pope put this First Lady into a new category of roving goodwill ambassador.

In the late summer of 1985, in the middle of our plans for the Reagan-Gorbachev summit in Geneva, Mexico City was hit with a severe earthquake. Mrs. Reagan debated whether a goodwill trip would be useful. The Mexicans appeared ambivalent about accepting assistance and friendship visits. Finally on twenty-four hours' notice she decided to accept the invitation of President Miguel de la Madrid to visit and express her country's concern. She took a check for one million dollars, a first installment of U.S. aid and was accompanied by Peter MacPherson, director of the Agency for International Development, and Elliot Abrams, Assistant Secretary of State for Latin America. Abrams and MacPherson briefed her on the way down to Mexico so she would be knowledgeable about the extent of the devastation but she was firm about the nature of her trip; she came to express friendship, not as an official delegate.

In November 1985, the Reagans went to Geneva to meet with the Soviet General Secretary Mikhail Gorbachev. In some ways publicity in the West surrounding the meetings of the two public wives surpassed the level of interest in the meetings of the two leaders. This was especially

*M*uch public attention was focused on Mrs. Reagan and Mrs. Gorbachev while the President and the Soviet General Secretary were holding their historic meeting in Geneva in 1985.

true when the official meetings were under a news blackout.

The American First Lady pursued a schedule typical for her: a visit to a drug center in Lausanne, a trip with schoolchildren on Lake Geneva, a scenic tour of a well-preserved old village, and the dedication of a new International Red Cross building. Then came reciprocal teas with Mrs. Gorbachev. The two first wives talked of their own countries and confirmed their interest in peace. Mrs. Gorbachev plied Mrs. Reagan with a bit of the party line but that was to be expected. When the Reagans and the Gorbachevs dined together there was an air of guarded cordiality. There was little doubt that while the first wives didn't forge policy they played a part in its drama.

The question of cost for value received surfaces every time the President and First Lady travel abroad. Their trips abroad undoubtedly cost the taxpayer a great deal. In the case of Mrs. Reagan's solo trips to London, Monaco, Italy, and Mexico, the State Department absorbed the expenses, the largest of which was for air travel. Manpower costs are fixed and added assistance is provided by nonreimbursed volunteers. Housing expenses for the First Lady are usually minimal. For the staff, hotel rates are negotiated annually and are significantly lower than those a tourist would pay.

A public attitude of skepticism has surfaced as a result of these trips that foreign policy and public diplomacy should be conducted by elected officials and government officeholders, not First Ladies. Nancy Reagan seems acutely aware of this and steers clear of discussing or even appearing to debate foreign policy on these trips. There remains, however, a basic value in a First Lady's ability to create goodwill for the United States through travel or other diplomatic missions. A similar value is understood by British politicians who defend the royal allowance as, pound for pound, a good investment in trade and tourism. Perhaps if they don't now, in the future the American people will more fully accept a globe-trotting First Lady, styled as diplomatic envoy of the President. A future First Lady may even have to count a negative cost to her public image should she choose to stay home and not pursue a course of public diplomacy.

Diplomacy is the art of talk, negotiations, and building channels of communication and trust between people — especially people of different nations. In this context the First Lady could play an increasingly important role — a role with significant opportunities to contribute to international cooperation and world peace. Whether it's seating herself between diplomats whose countries were at war with each other as Dolley Madison did, or attending the inauguration of a president in a developing nation as a representative of the American President, as Pat Nixon did, or discussing international economics with kings during a world war as Eleanor Roosevelt did — the American First Lady can be a potent diplomatic force. Her presence is often enough to indicate the interest of the United States in the affairs of those countries she might visit. A First Lady may help open the doors to peace, stronger ties with our allies, and more effective global communication among world leaders.

*T*he Reagans, awed by the memories of this tragic place, observe the Hebrew-inscribed wall at the Bergen-Belsen memorial to Holocaust victims on their visit to Germany in May 1985. (overleaf)

אימפּאראבל
ט, טשישע
העלם יידישן
ר - 1945 - 1939
און אידישע
ראך
ראר
וואַ

"TO THE MEMORY OF ALL
WHO DIED IN THIS PLAC[E]

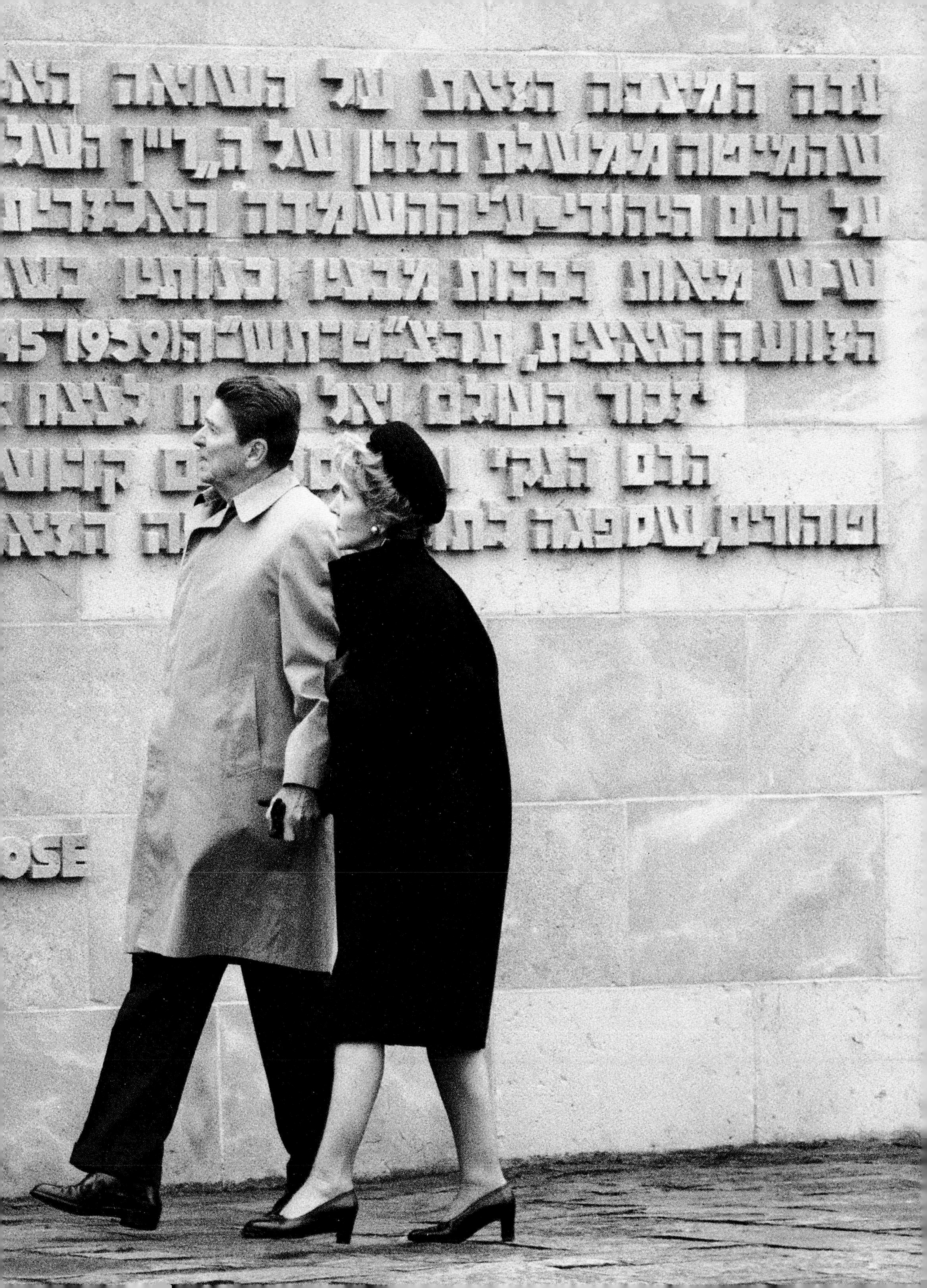

Hostess for a Nation

In the beginning the job of First Lady was primarily social. The millions of visitors to the White House, whether on public tours or as guests at state dinners, expect to experience something special. To help provide this special experience has always been the responsibility of the First Lady and her staff. But First Ladies have not always been comfortable fulfilling the social demands of the job, nor have they always been adept at entertaining.

When Martha Washington arrived in the capital of her day, she found a New York mansion on Cherry Street filled with assistants and household staff to help her get through the heavy social calendar already planned for her. At least two of the first couple's many nephews were appointed to escort Martha Washington to social functions when the President was not available. To help her plan parties she called upon the President's right hand man Tobias Lear and the first official presidential steward, Samuel Fraunces. When the capital was moved to Philadelphia, Fraunces moved with the Washingtons.

The involvement of family members in planning and acting as hostesses at White House social events began with Elizabeth Monroe's dependency on her daughter Eliza Hay. Eliza even planned the wedding of her sister, Maria, the first presidential daughter to be married in the White House. Family responsibility for White House social events continued throughout the nineteenth century. John Tyler's many daughters assisted as social aides. Sarah Polk's nieces helped the First Lady with invitations and seating charts. Jane Pierce's best friend and aunt-by-marriage, Abby Kent Means, aided the First Lady in all aspects of hostessing and served as surrogate First Lady during the first two years of the Pierce Administration. The niece of Lucy Hayes not only enjoyed social-season receptions at the White House, but helped plan them. Caroline Harrison's niece had a similar role. The

King Juan Carlos of Spain and Queen Sophia entertain President and Mrs. Reagan at a state dinner at the Royal Palace in Madrid in May 1985. The hospitality was reciprocated at a White House luncheon in 1987.

bevy of daughters, daughters-in-law, cousins, and sisters who helped as social secretaries often lived right in the family quarters at the White House.

During Thomas Jefferson's administration Dolley Madison, the wife of Secretary of State James Madison, functioned as official White House hostess. She initiated a grand but warm style of entertaining, appearing at parties in satin and velvet turbans with ostrich plumes. Dolley was well prepared when her turn came to fill the role of national hostess as the wife of the President. When the snobbish wife of the British ambassador rudely commented that Dolley Madison's serving buffet-style dinners from groaning tables was "more like a harvest home supper than the entertainment of a Secretary of State," indomitable Dolley defended her style as truly American. "Abundance is preferable to elegance," Dolley insisted, ". . . and as the profusion so repugnant to foreign customs rises from the happy circumstances of the abundance and prosperity of the country, I don't hesitate to

Carriages pull up to the North Portico of the White House to pick up guests after a reception in January 1886. Today, most guests arrive and depart from the East entrance of the mansion.

sacrifice the delicacy of European taste for the less elegant but more liberal fashion of Virginia."

Few First Ladies have been as successful a hostess as Dolley Madison. She used entertaining for political purposes and set a remarkable pace of socializing. Dolley broke all previous records as a popular hostess of the people. She often led curious tourists through the state rooms herself. Once when interrupted at breakfast by two women who had come from the far West to see her, Mrs. Madison graciously rose to greet them, kissed them, and spent time explaining how the house was run. But the legend of Dolley Madison began at her public "crushes" — receptions to which any citizen with an introduction could attend. She served whiskey punch, wore those outrageously plumed turbans, festooned gold chains around her neck and arms, highly rouged her cheeks, and moved informally through "the mob" as she affectionately called the guests. Needless to say, she was the star attraction, someone described her as "every inch a queen."

Her popularity may simply have been due to her genuine warmth and love of people — regardless of their racial, religious, or economic background. Because some of her guests felt uncomfortable in formal settings, Dolley had her own special ways to help them feel at ease. She carried around with her a copy of *Don Quixote* and when she spotted timid wallflowers in corners, she came up and asked if they had read the book. If they had, she asked their opinions of it; if they hadn't, she admitted that she hadn't either, having been too busy to get through it. It was her own brand of icebreaker.

Mrs. Madison often invited her husband's most bitter political rivals to dinner. Not only were they flattered, but under Dolley's spell they frequently softened towards her husband. It was no mistake that at formal dinners President Madison placed her, and not himself, at the head of the table next to key statesmen.

Dolley Madison's staggering success as hostess placed a nearly impossible burden on her successors. Since none could duplicate her skills, each developed her own style as hostess. Eliz-

abeth Monroe instituted European-style entertaining. She received and spoke to her guests as they came through a formal receiving line. At her dinners, with the newly purchased, shimmering gold plateau centerpiece spanning the length of the long table, guests were served in the English style with waiters passing each course. Louisa Adams, an accomplished musician, often played the harp to entertain her guests after dinner. Mrs. Adams, the only European-born First Lady, held several highly successful receptions for the visiting Marquis de Lafayette.

Julia Gardiner Tyler initiated a rather scandalous form of greeting her guests. Seated on a thronelike chair on a raised dais, wearing a crown of bugle beads and feathers and surrounded by twelve "vestal virgins" in identical white dresses,

*B*ritish-born, though half American, Mrs. John Quincy Adams proved a charming hostess, often entertaining guests by playing the harp. Her hostessing skills had been developed as a diplomat's wife.

Entertaining in the White House in the early years presented challenges. In Abigail Adams' time there was no running water; it was hauled from half a mile away. Not until the 1850s was a kitchen stove installed.

Mrs. Tyler bowed to her guests as their names were called out loudly by an aide. It was Versailles on the Potomac.

Her immediate successor, Sarah Polk, a religious zealot, wiped the mark of Julia completely away from the role of hostess. Mrs. Polk refused to allow dancing after dinner, even banned music, and served no after-dinner refreshments. Wine was served at formal dinners but at no time during the Polk regime was hard liquor served. Sarah Polk was not altogether unprogressive however. She approved the installation of gaslights in the state rooms, but she asked that candles remain in the Blue Room. During the very first reception held after the new lights were installed, they all went out. But the Blue Room remained lighted — thanks to the perceptive First Lady.

Other First Ladies concentrated less on entertainment and more on the food and drink.

Abigail Fillmore ordered the first modern cooking stove for the White House kitchens. Lucy Hayes, like Sarah Polk, refused to allow liquor to be served in the White House. Her advocacy of temperance earned her the nickname "Lemonade Lucy." Mary Arthur McElroy, serving as First Lady for her widowed brother, President Chester Arthur, held special ladies' luncheons and teas at which she used different pastel colors as themes for different events.

Edith Roosevelt introduced music at her weekly receptions. She invited famous musicians to entertain her guests and she showcased such outstanding talents as Pablo Casals. Mrs. Roosevelt also sponsored the first coming-out party in the White House, the debut of her stepdaughter Alice Roosevelt. Years later, as Mrs. Nicholas Longworth, Alice wistfully complained that the party wasn't a success because her stepmother hadn't allowed champagne to be served.

Florence Harding loved the outdoors and used the White House grounds for spring and summer entertaining. While the Marine band played and the fountains danced, women in flapper dresses and men in boaters enjoyed the newly landscaped south lawn. Because it was during prohibition, Mrs. Harding served a variety of fruit punches called "squalls" in such flavors as banana, mint, and lemon.

At first Eleanor Roosevelt was bothered by time-consuming social responsibilities; she preferred to spend her time writing a daily newspaper column, giving public lectures and radio broadcasts, and traveling. But she soon developed a healthy respect for the political and

Eleanor Roosevelt consults with Malvina Thompson, left, her personal secretary, and Edith Helm, her social secretary. In the first year alone, Mrs. Roosevelt received over 300,000 pieces of mail.

diplomatic values of White House entertaining. "I think," she wrote, "Edith Helm (her social secretary) often felt I did not take enough interest in the social side of the White House duties, but at that time they seemed to me rather unimportant; indeed, there never came a point when I felt the world was sufficiently stable for us to take the time to think very seriously about purely social matters. Certain duties, however, which I thought at first were useless burdens I

In 1978, outdoor entertaining took a new turn at the first White House Jazz Festival. One of the many jazz greats who performed was 95-year-old Eubie Blake, who played ragtime for Jimmy and Rosalynn Carter.

Lady Bird Johnson, thrust precipitously into the role of presidential hostess, meets with Queen Fredericka of Greece, CIA Director John McCone and Princess Beatrix of the Netherlands after the funeral of John F. Kennedy.

later grew to realize had meaning and value. For instance, the teas. It seemed to me utterly futile to receive anywhere from five hundred to a thousand people of an afternoon, shake hands with them. . .I soon discovered that. . .the White House has a deep significance. It's a place where the people's hospitality is dispensed. . .it is with a sense of ownership that the citizens of the United States walk through the dignified and beautiful rooms. To many people the White House symbolizes government and though standing and shaking hands for an hour or two is not an inspiring occupation, still I think it well worth while. At the first few receptions of each season my arms ached, my shoulders ached, my back ached and my knees and feet seemed to belong to someone else."

Mamie Eisenhower loved playing the role of hostess, particularly on holidays. At Christmas she decked the columns on the state floor with holly and had carols piped throughout the house. At Halloween she hung paper skeletons and witches from the ceilings and placed pumpkins and cornstalks in the entrance hall. At Easter it

was chirping bird sounds in the dining room and colored eggs with bunnies and chicks sticking their heads out.

During many presidential terms, the duties of White House social secretary were combined with those of the First Lady's personal assistant and press secretary. Only with Letitia Baldridge, Mrs. Kennedy's assistant, were these responsibilities consolidated into one bona fide position. In planning her dual role as social secretary/ staff chief, Tish Baldridge consulted the women who had been assistants to Mamie Eisenhower and Eleanor Roosevelt and she found a need for greater coordination of staff functions.

What others had to learn about the value of White House social events came almost instinctively to Jacqueline Kennedy. During the Kennedy Administration, invitations to the White House, always considered a plum, were more eagerly sought than ever before. Both of Mrs. Kennedy's social secretaries — Letitia Baldridge and Nancy Tuckerman — recalled the First Lady's sense of imagination in planning special events. Mrs. Kennedy did away with the

E-shaped table used by the Eisenhowers for state dinners and revived Thomas Jefferson's round tables, considered to provide more democratic and intimate seating. After-dinner entertainment featured the lively arts, and a special stage was constructed for those performances at the north end of the East Room. Nobel poets recited their works and the New York Shakespearean theatre performed excerpts from plays. One evening featured a ballet performance. Only Jacqueline Kennedy could have persuaded Pablo Casals to play his cello at the White House after he vowed never to perform in public in a country that recognized Franco's government in Spain.

Pat Nixon instituted a series of "Evenings at the White House" that coincided with the bicentennial celebration in 1976. One of the most memorable was the recreation of the then-popular musical *1776* in which John Adams and Thomas Jefferson were characters. Another time Mrs. Nixon turned the mansion into an art gallery displaying the work of prominent American artists. Betty Ford added her own touch to White House dinners by placing American heritage craft centerpieces — no two alike — as centerpieces on the tables.

One of the most enjoyable events on the White House calendar is the Easter Egg Roll. Tens of thousands of children are admitted to the south lawn to compete in egg-rolling contests, to hunt for hidden wooden eggs, and to be entertained by magic acts, singers, and clowns. The

While Pat Nixon hugs one of the children of diplomatic families invited to the annual White House Christmas party, dancers from the Washington School of Ballet, who had performed in the Nutcracker Suite, gather around.

event was started by Dolley Madison at the Capitol; but it moved to the White House during the term of Lucy Hayes. During the two world wars, the Easter Egg Roll was suspended, but Mamie Eisenhower revived the event in the fifties.

Nancy Reagan attended the Egg Roll as a child, during the Coolidge Administration and as First Lady she turned it into a more ambitious event. She imported the best of Broadway plays, like *Annie*, to be performed during the day's festivities and one year the Corcoran School of Art created life-size color cutout figures from *Alice in Wonderland*, with faces of famous political figures.

A tradition of less-formal entertaining be-gan when Jacqueline Kennedy held an occasional state dinner on the south lawn or in the Rose Garden. This became a regular September institution during the Reagan Administration. I distinctly remember Mrs. Reagan's first experience with the alfresco dinners in 1982. Thousands of tiny white lights dazzled guests at dinner in the Rose Garden, but it was so dark on the south lawn that waiters passing after-dinner drinks repeatedly collided with the guests! That problem was remedied the following September with torches that lined the driveway and provided additional lighting. Outdoor entertaining has also included informal picnics. California barbecues for members of Congress were always a favorite of the Reagans.

Surprised tourists visiting the first floor state rooms at the White House encounter Rosalynn Carter in the Blue Room. She often came down unannounced to welcome tourists.

Nancy Reagan talks with young culinary students who prepared the food for a reception for Americans living in Paris at the Petit Palais signaling the opening of a 1982 exhibition of American Impressionists.

Today the social office of the White House is an institution unto itself. I first realized that when I watched White House chef Henry Haller and his assistants begin in August to bake the hundreds of pounds of Christmas cookies and fruitcakes needed for the thousands of special visitors to the White House at Christmastime. Christmas at the White House is a rewarding but demanding time for the social office. Planning for a steady procession of receptions for military and staff families, the elderly, and the general public begins six months in advance. For the three weeks prior to Christmas the social office manages up to three events a day most of which are hosted personally by the First Lady.

As hostess to the nation, the First Lady's guests fall into two categories: public visitors who come to the White House on tour or for a special occasion and guests invited specifically by the President and First Lady. The public visits the mansion at the rate of a million a year. Most of them come on general public, congressional, or special tours of the ground floor and state rooms of the White House. Guided tours are provided by a uniformed division of the U.S. Secret Service and the guides happily dispense trivia on how many bathrooms and sets of china there are in the executive mansion. A visitors office in the east wing handles requests for special group passes, is responsible for daily tours, and plans and manages the First Lady's special garden tours in the spring and fall.

Visitors on public tours talk readily of the

pride they feel in their country when they visit the White House. The way the White House is maintained, the furnishings, the flowers, the grounds all reflect on a First Lady even though she never puts a mop to the floor. In recent administrations, the maintenance of the White House has been the responsibility of the chief usher and his staff. The overall appearance is the result of cooperation between the First Lady and the chief usher — during my tenure and in several previous administrations, Rex Scouten. On any given day, Mrs. Reagan might meet with Rex several times. They collaborate on repair and refurbishment as well as on purchases of linens and flowers, all part of the chief usher's responsibilities.

Today, the White House social office is responsible for guests who are invited to the White House. During the years 1982-86, under a succession of three social secretaries: Muffie Brandon, Gahl Hodges Burt, and Linda Faulkner, the social office created and managed an average of three hundred events a year. The First Lady set the standards for entertaining and these women came up with a steady supply of creative ideas, guest lists that were interesting and appropriate, and innovative entertainment suggestions. They worked closely with the First Lady to think of enjoyable, interesting events and then with her approval and watchful eye carried through with the management of each from the draft guest list to saying goodnight to the guests when they departed the White House.

First Ladies and Others Who Served as Public Hostess

Administration	Wife	Late Wife	Daughter	Daughter-In-Law	Niece	President's Sister	Others/Cabinet Wife
Washington 1789–1797	Martha						
J. Adams 1797–1801	Abigail						
Jefferson 1801–1809		Martha	Martha Randolph				Dolley Madison (Cabinet wife)
Madison 1809–1817	Dolley						
Monroe 1817–1825	Elizabeth		Eliza Hay				
J.Q. Adams 1825–1829	Louisa						
Jackson 1829–1837		Rachel		Sarah York Jackson	Emily Donelson		Peggy Eaton (Cabinet wife)
Van Buren 1837–1841		Hannah		Angelica Van Buren			
W. Harrison 1841	Anna (not present)			Jane Irwin Harrison			Jane Findlay (Daughter-in-law's aunt)
Tyler 1841–1845	Letitia Julia		Letty Tyler Semple	Priscilla Cooper Tyler			

Lucretia Garfield

Martha Jefferson Randolph

Dolley Madison

Administration	Wife	Late Wife	Daughter	Daughter-In-Law	Niece	President's Sister	Others/ Cabinet Wife
Polk 1845–1849	Sarah						
Taylor 1849–1850	Margaret		Elizabeth Taylor Bliss				
Fillmore 1850–1853	Abigail		Mary Abigail Fillmore				
Pierce 1853–1857	Jane						Abigail Kent Means (Mrs. Pierce's aunt)
Buchanan 1857–1861	(bachelor)				Harriet Lane		
Lincoln 1861–1865	Mary						
A. Johnson 1865–1869	Eliza		Martha Patterson, Mary Stover				
Grant 1869–1877	Julia						
Hayes 1877–1881	Lucy						
Garfield 1881	Lucretia						

Harriet Lane

Lucy Hayes

Eliza Johnson

Administration	Wife	Late Wife	Daughter	Daughter-In-Law	Niece	President's Sister	Others/Cabinet Wife
Arthur 1881–1885		Ellen				Mary Arthur McElroy	
Cleveland 1885–1889 1893–1897	Frances (m. 1886)					Rose Cleveland	
B. Harrison 1889–1893	Caroline		Mary McKee				
McKinley 1897–1901	Ida						
T. Roosevelt 1901–1909	Edith						
Taft 1909–1913	Helen		Helen Taft				Maria Moore (Mrs. Taft's sister)
Wilson 1913–1921	Ellen Edith		Margaret Wilson				Helen Bones (President's cousin)
Harding 1921–1923	Florence						
Coolidge 1923–1929	Grace						
Hoover 1929–1933	Lou						

Hostess for a Nation 82

Frances Cleveland

Grace Coolidge

Ida McKinley

Administration	Wife	Late Wife	Daughter	Daughter-In-Law	Niece	President's Sister	Others/ Cabinet Wife
F. Roosevelt 1933–1945	Eleanor		Anna Roosevelt Dall Boettiger				
Truman 1945–1953	Bess						
Eisenhower 1953–1961	Mamie						
Kennedy 1961–1963	Jacqueline					Eunice Shriver (served on one state occasion)	
L. Johnson 1963–1969	Lady Bird						
Nixon 1969–1974	Patricia						
Ford 1974–1977	Betty						
Carter 1977–1981	Rosalynn						
Reagan 1981–	Nancy						

Betty Ford, Nancy Reagan, and Rosalynn Carter

Champion of Causes

Two basic and developing trends in American cultural history have helped promote the role of First Lady as a "public wife," given to public causes. First, Americans have an almost instinctive tendency to get involved, singularly or as a group, to fix a local community or national ill. Social historians have observed that Americans band together to raise a barn or to stop child labor practices. Since the beginnings of the nation, writers have commented on this inherent and typically American trait. Working for the public good is a political tradition practiced by Ben Franklin, Thomas Jefferson, and other Founding Fathers. Public figures have been expected to acknowledge that involvement in other people's troubles is what gives value to life.

The second trend has to do with the acceptance of women in the field of social work. Pioneering work in the tenement houses of Chicago in the late 1800s, the development of women's civic clubs and national sororities, and the increasing number of women attending college promoted women into the fray in the early twentieth century. The suffragette movement thrust many women into political activism and galvanized the thinking of many others about their value to their country and their community.

Although some early First Ladies adopted social causes, serious involvement as social activists came later and generally mirrored the evolving cultural and political profile of American women.

Ellen Wilson's concern moved her to become the first First Lady to take on a serious special project. Washington's streets were crisscrossed by scores of back alleys where thousands of the city's poor Black population lived in shanties. Mrs. Wilson, against the advice of some of the President's counselors, made it her goal to encourage congressional legislation to improve these dwellings. She took congressmen and debutantes alike by the hand and led them

O n a visit to an Oakland, California elementary school, Mrs. Reagan asked youngsters how they would respond to an offer of drugs. The "Just Say No" movement was borne out of their answer.

S ome First Ladies, like Lou Henry Hoover, continued championing their causes after their White House years. Here she receives her badge of office on becoming president of the Girl Scouts in 1935.

through alley homes. She attended social-service conferences and held dinners with federal legislators. Her "alley bill" was passed by Congress just days after her untimely death on August 6, 1914.

Other First Ladies have manifested social consciences during their White House years. Edith Roosevelt regularly sent personal checks to organizations which she read or heard were in need of financial assistance. Grace Coolidge volunteered many hours to the Red Cross. She particularly enjoyed helping wounded, maimed, and blinded veterans of the First World War; and she wore her own Grey Lady uniform to Red Cross events. During the Great Depression, Lou Hoover used her special project — the Girl Scouts — to mobilize volunteer youth groups to seek out the families in their communities who most needed financial assistance, extra food, and other help. Mrs. Hoover effectively used the radio to plead with the American people to identify and help those in need. If Mrs. Hoover's approach to the depression was volunteerism, Eleanor Roosevelt's was government assistance. Mrs. Roosevelt was especially interested in social causes and justice. Whenever she was told about or read of an individual in need she sought to help them either personally or through a government agency. Her cousin Alice Longworth once joked that "never has a woman so comforted the distressed and so distressed the comfortable."

The feminist movement of the past thirty years may have had less radical impact on the office of First Lady than might be expected, however. Polls taken during 1983–85 reveal that a very traditional role continues to be the one most accepted for First Ladies today. For example, Richard Wirthlin's survey data shows Nancy Reagan's popularity to be based primarily on her concern and care for her husband and then on her involvement in a far-reaching social cause.

While Americans have come to expect a First Lady to do more than take care of her family and pour tea in the afternoon for White House guests, acceptance teeters between too little work on a cause and too much. Americans want their First Ladies dished up attractive, bright, serious, and active; but they don't want to hear about them too much. A degree of mystery and disengagement seems to enchant the public. Perhaps because the public is terribly protective of its vote and the power of that vote they feel a certain ownership of those elected. This extends to a spouse of any elected official as well. Voters send up warning signals when they think a spouse may eclipse the power of, or even strongly influence, the individual chosen by the voters to represent them.

Occupants of the White House almost always comment on the fishbowllike existence there. Their personal private lives become public, open to scrutiny of every kind from political to romantic. Once a First Lady enters the White House there are few ways of escaping a thorough and constant examination by the public.

It was always interesting to me to pass through a crowd when Mrs. Reagan was delivering a speech and listen to the comments about her. Invariably they began with her being "too thin" or "too glamorous," and usually they ended with "Can she really be that sincere?" Skepticism and politics seem to be inextricably linked; perhaps that's why politicians don't rank high on the list of those Americans trust most.

The omnipresent cycle of campaigning and image marketing must breed distrust and skepticism. After more than six years of campaigning against drug abuse, Nancy Reagan's efforts to help wipe out the disease are considered by some to be just a public relations ploy.

I can understand why Nancy Reagan watchers might have been suspicious in her first year in the White House. Such doubts were even heard among White House staffers again around the time of the 1984 re-election campaign. Would Nancy Reagan continue her antidrug crusade during a second presidential term, or, satisfied with her husband's reaching a milestone in American history, a two-term presidency, would she abandon her cause for more comfort and her personal friends?

There is little doubt that Mrs. Reagan's drug crusade began in 1979 when campaign advisors urged the First Lady to become identified with an issue on which she could find common concern with the average American. Beautification, mental health, preservation, volunteerism, or even women's rights, all issues chosen by earlier First Ladies and by then successful projects, were the kinds of activities the political advisors had in mind.

But Nancy Reagan had something else in her mind. Her community service had always centered around hospitals. Growing up the daughter of a prominent Chicago neurosurgeon, and one who, she told me often, took her to the hospital to observe, she developed a comfortableness in a hospital setting. During college she served as a nurse's aide and as a governor's wife made a practice of visiting hospitals. In fact, during one such visit, to the Pomona State Hospital, she discovered the Foster Grandparent Program, which brings the elderly and the young together in support of each other, and which she has promoted nationally.

For one who never liked hospitals and

Lucy Hayes, remembered as Lemonade Lucy because she forbade the serving of alcohol at White House functions, was an independent, well-educated woman. She blended her feminist image with traditional activities.

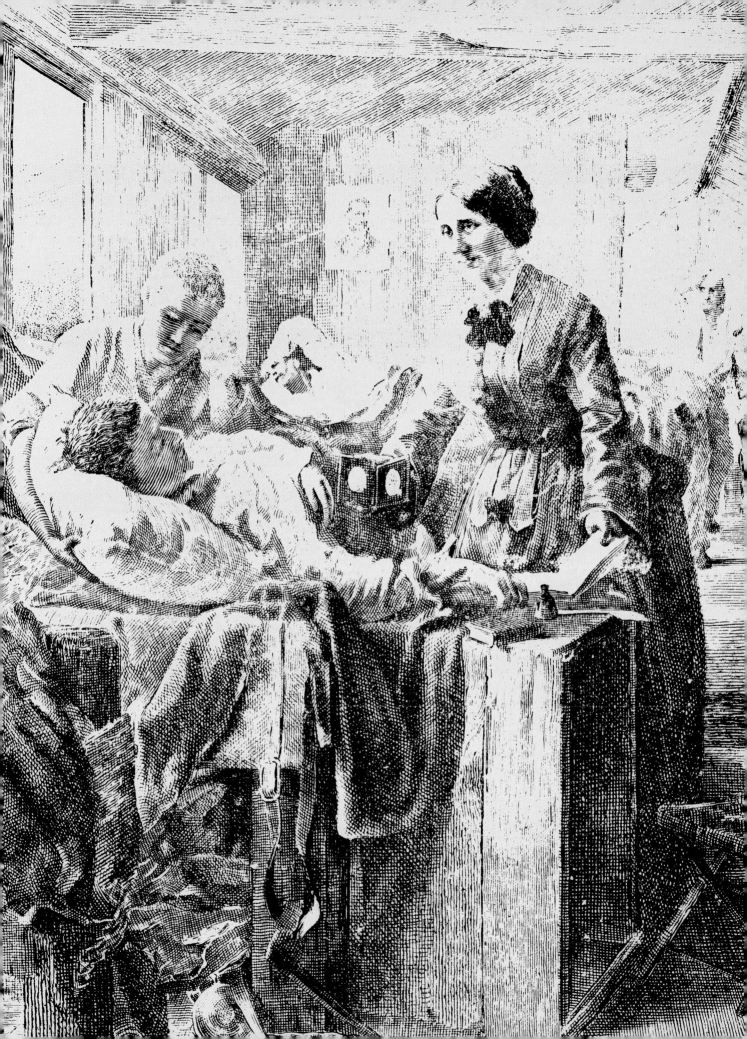

especially intensive care wards, it was hard for me when she would leave the scheduled tour and beat a path directly to the intensive care unit to talk to anxious family members and patients. As an example of just how comfortable she was in hospitals, during her father's prolonged illness prior to his death she lived in a room adjacent to his at the Scottsdale Memorial Hospital. Her staff stayed in a motel across the street. It seemed to me that I could always detect a feeling of fulfillment from her hospital visits. It must have something to do with being a doctor's daughter.

I remember once trying to give her a dose of her own medicine. We were to visit the Royal College of Surgeons where she was to receive an honorary degree being bestowed posthumously on her father Loyal Davis. On my advance trip to the college the dean took me on a tour that included a research laboratory filled with cadavers and pickled brains, livers, and other body parts donated for research. At last, I thought, I would test the First Lady's ability to walk graciously through a depressing site. Somehow the college officials did not want the First Lady's visit to Dublin to be marked with a front-page newspaper picture of her examining corpses, so my plan was foiled.

To choose a cause was a political necessity and Nancy Reagan, ignoring the counsel of some advisors, chose drug abuse as a cause to tackle — perhaps because it was health related and because it was a serious problem. How serious a problem it was she really didn't know. Initially she knew only what any parent living through the drug culture of the sixties, especially in California, would know. Instinctively, though, she knew this would be something she could relate to. She also knew enough about the drug-related deaths of children of friends to know this was a serious epidemic that needed to be addressed and a problem she was already concerned about.

That she chose a cause in 1979 was part of

*M*rs. Reagan addresses the first world-wide conference of First Ladies on the drug abuse problem in 1985. Eighteen First Ladies from around the world attended the two-day event.

the campaign; and, in that, it was a political choice. Her husband was running for office and she was attempting to become First Lady. By 1979, supporting a cause was a given, a necessity. What happened after that was that the more immersed in the issue she became, the more it overwhelmed her, impressed her. The problem drew her in. It changed her. In the beginning I'm not sure how deeply she thought she would become engaged in the fight against drugs. But listening for hours at a time to the horrors young people faced drew her in. It was this soul-to-soul communication that young people saw and admired in her. It provided the glue, the bond between the First Lady and young people. I often stood by and watched it happen.

One of Nancy Reagan's predecessors said, "I wonder how anyone who reaches middle age can bear it if she cannot feel, on looking back, that whatever mistakes she has made, she has on the whole lived for others and not herself." Ellen Wilson, Woodrow Wilson's first wife, wrote that after making a study of Washington's alley people. To tackle the problem of inadequate housing, she met with various welfare organiza-

*T*he golden glow of daffodils lights up a strip of parkland in Washington, D.C. as Lady Bird Johnson chats with admiring passers-by. Her work at beautifying America has left a lasting legacy.

*H*undreds of foster grandparents from the Washington, D.C.-area gather for a party on the south lawn of the White House for the publication of Mrs. Reagan's book, To Love a Child. *(overleaf)*

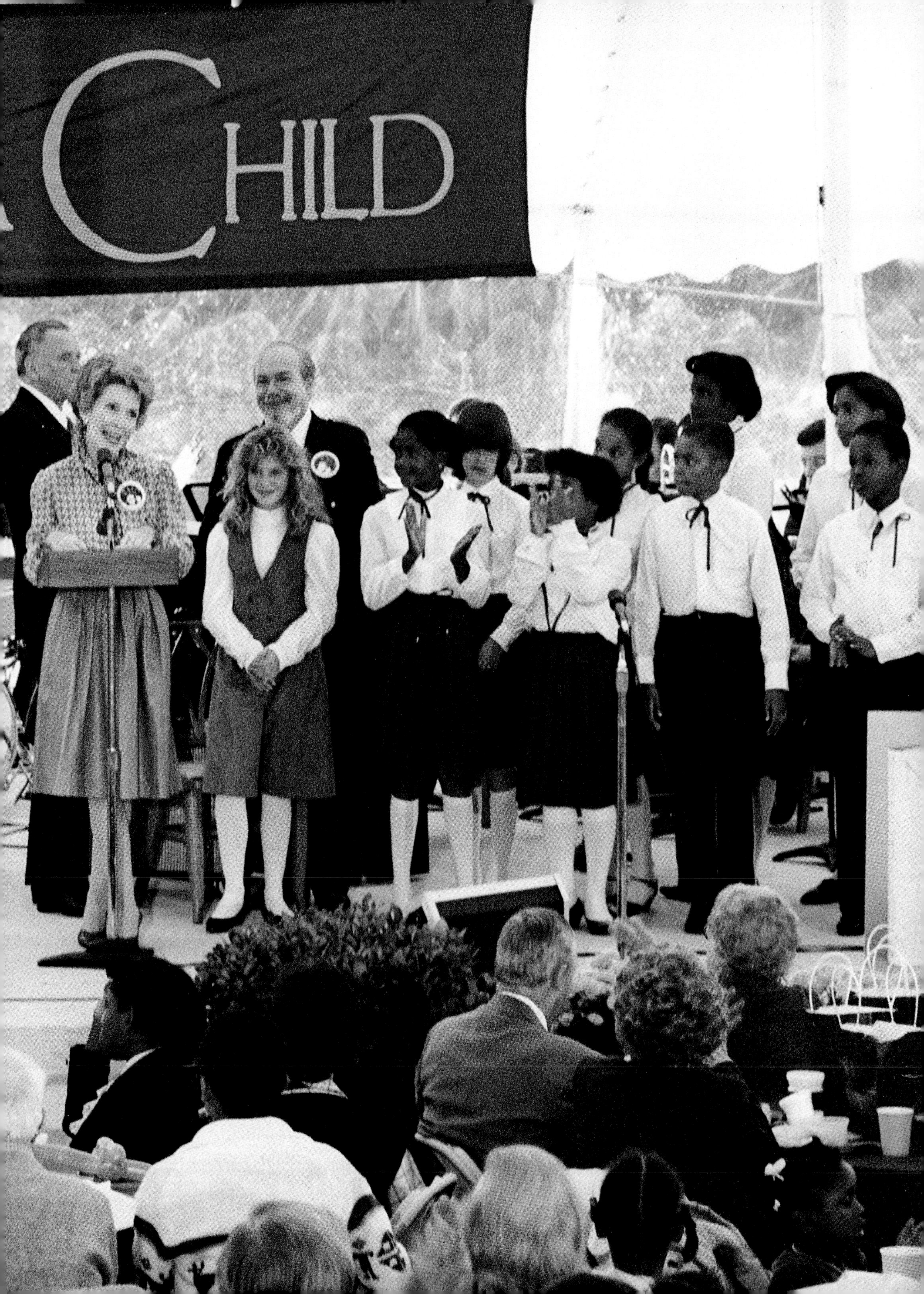
CHILD

*R*epresentatives of the Visiting Nurses Association watch Grace Coolidge cut the anniversary cake to celebrate their founding. Mrs. Coolidge sometimes used sign language, which she learned working with the deaf.

tions, consulted experts on urban development, and held conferences and meetings to try to effect change. Mrs. Wilson's well-coordinated campaign had the help of social worker Mrs. Archibald Hopkins and was one of the first formal projects to be sponsored by a First Lady. One of its results was the Slum Clearance Act of 1915 which helped reduce urban squalor.

Before Ellen Wilson there had been sporadic involvement in substantive issues including Dolley Madison's efforts to improve orphan care in Washington. Harriet Lane worked with social reformers to improve the education of native Americans; Caroline Harrison campaigned for equal education for women; Florence Harding investigated the conditions of disabled veterans; Grace Coolidge helped the deaf; and Lou Hoover had her hands full with depression-caused projects including helping the unemployed in any way she could.

With 1933 and the ascent of Eleanor Roose-velt, First Ladies' causes took on new seriousness. She became involved in many causes and spoke openly about them at press conferences — the first at which a First Lady went on the record, permitting herself to be quoted directly — and in her frequent speeches and daily column. She was the first to undertake significant causes on a national level rather than attack problems associated only with the nation's capital. She understood and used the media well enough to realize that while her good works would sometimes receive national attention they could be knocked off the front page by presidential politics and world news.

Eleanor Roosevelt's projects caused quite a bit of controversy. Working in a less tolerant time, assisting poor Blacks was a particularly sensitive issue, even to her husband's advisors. Eleanor Roosevelt paid no attention to critics and continued to speak out against the inequality of the races, focusing on the issue of education for minorities. Her conduit for this was Mary Bethune, a nationally recognized Black educator whose family had experienced slavery firsthand. Much of Mrs. Roosevelt's work was behind the scenes, but her most visible, and perhaps most famous, act on behalf of civil rights was resigning from the Daughters of the American Revolution when the organization refused to allow Black singer Marian Anderson to perform in their concert hall. Mrs. Roosevelt then arranged for Anderson to sing for the public on Easter Sunday at the Lincoln Memorial.

An important distinction could be made between Eleanor Roosevelt's initial motivation to become involved in causes and Nancy Reagan's. Mrs. Roosevelt became involved because she was motivated by an issue while Mrs. Reagan's initial involvement was more political. But whatever their reasons, both became committed to the subject, the issues, and the victims. They are vastly different women and both have been the subject of keen and intense observation; but in their own ways they stand for what the American woman can achieve.

Just as many observers were skeptical of Mrs. Roosevelt in her day as have been of Mrs. Reagan more recently. Reporters during the Roosevelt years asked if they were being used by a keenly political, energetic, and intelligent woman to boost her image as First Lady. Mrs. Roosevelt's continued support of important projects after her husband's death caused her to be named repeatedly as the most admired First Lady. With time for reflection, Mrs. Roosevelt's projects here and abroad to help the downtrodden and the war torn receive supportive reviews and command praise from many world leaders as well as many Americans.

If Eleanor Roosevelt knew how to use press briefings, newsreels, and a newspaper column to express an opinion, Nancy Reagan knew how to use television and the increased demand for news by the White House and national press corps. Wherever Mrs. Reagan went on drug abuse business, whether to the Vatican or to Cennikor Drug Treatment Center in Denver, she was trailed by reporters and cameras. She may not

have appeared on the national news every evening but her trips were all recorded by local media. Both Mrs. Roosevelt and Mrs. Reagan, however, had a healthy skepticism of the media and both insisted on some private meetings on issues and some visits to hospitals without having the media present.

Between Eleanor Roosevelt and Nancy Reagan other First Ladies had to deal with the national media's voracious appetite for personal details of family life and lack of enthusiasm for causes. Mrs. Nixon's work to promote volunteerism went all but unnoticed because the press corps found it boring. Lady Bird's beautification project was often overshadowed by anti-Vietnam demonstrations. Even Jackie Kennedy's now-hailed restoration of the White House would have gone largely unnoticed had it not been for the Edward R. Murrow tour of the state rooms led by Mrs. Kennedy. The show was watched by

Eleanor Roosevelt said of herself, "I have no talents, experience, no training for anything." Here, at her Hyde Park home, she hosts a picnic for students at the Harbor Shore Labor School.

millions and is still regarded as a television classic. Rosalynn Carter was serious in her pursuit of solutions to the nation's mental health problems. However, her involvement in some areas of government policy distracted media attention from her efforts for mental health program reform.

There were many efforts to distract Mrs. Reagan from her work on drugs. Most of the distractions were worthy causes. First Ladies are always expected to sponsor certain projects, many handed down by previous First Ladies. Any First Lady is expected to work with and answer the requests of cabinet wives and congressional spouses. Children's hospitals, local museums, and municipal groups all clamor for the First Lady's endorsement. Then there are national causes — many looking for sponsorship by the First Lady. When I was chief of staff Mrs.

In preparation for her historic television Tour of the White House, *Mrs. Kennedy discusses with Charles Collingwood of CBS, the noteworthy objects and pieces of furniture to be featured on the show.*

Reagan received hundreds of requests each month to serve as honorary chairman or patron of benefits and national causes. At one point Mrs. Reagan served as patron of about a hundred organizations. Finally the staff developed a list of criteria for accepting invitations so the organizers would not be personally offended when they received a regret.

Mrs. Reagan tried to limit her involvement on an honorary level to organizations that are national in scope and related to her work on drugs or cultural issues. Some exceptions were made for Washington organizations such as the National Symphony Orchestra and Children's Hospital. Other community leaders found it hard to understand why Mrs. Reagan could not add their cause to her list, but ultimately her acceptance was more meaningful if she could *participate* in some way. Many fund raisers feel that a commitment from a First Lady to appear at their benefit or in their advertising campaigns is a guarantee of higher level of donations. The legal advisor to the President ruled that a First Lady could not endorse any commercial venture and that automatically eliminated a number of requests from corporate endorsement seekers. A small sampling of Mrs. Reagan's honorary chairmanships during my tenure included:

> Juvenile Diabetes Foundation
> National Heart Association
> National Symphony Orchestra
> Meridian House International
> Girl Scouts of America
> Phoenix House Drug Abuse Center
> Salvation Army
> Multiple Sclerosis Association
> National Federation of Parents for Drug
>   Free Youth
> Joffrey Ballet
> Covenant House

Some national causes, such as the Girl Scouts, received special attention. In 1984 Mrs. Reagan hosted the Girl Scouts' birthday party in the East Room of the White House. Chef Haller made a birthday cake shaped like a huge Girl Scout cookie; and after blowing out the candles,

*P*resident Jimmy Carter kisses wife Rosalynn after she delivered the report on the President's Commission on Mental Health. She also worked with those who were concerned with women's issues and problems of the elderly.

the First Lady was awarded a merit badge for her work in drug abuse.

While Mrs. Kennedy, Mrs. Johnson, and Mrs. Carter all used experts to advise them on their principal projects, Mrs. Reagan was the first to hire staff members expert in the field of her cause. Although Ann Wrobleski was hired in 1981 as a special projects generalist, she quickly became knowledgeable in drug abuse education, prevention, and rehabilitation. In 1986 she became an assistant secretary for international narcotics matters at the U.S. Department of State. Following Ann's departure Ken Barun, a reformed drug addict himself and former president of Cennikor Foundation, one of the largest drug rehabilitation centers in the country, was hired to assist the First Lady with her drug abuse campaign. Ken added the credibility that only a

former drug user could and helped increase Mrs. Reagan's awareness about the causes of drug abuse and its effects on young people.

From 1982 to 1986 the First Lady's drug campaign was organized to have a special theme for each year. The pattern looked like this:

1982 — Focus on young people in treatment centers.

1983 — Use television to educate a larger audience.

1984 — Seek assistance from national organizations and service clubs to develop prevention and awareness programs.

1985 — Focus on international aspects of drugs.

1986 — Focus on effects of drug use on special groups such as teen mothers.

On the whole, Bess Truman stayed so much out of the limelight that she could go shopping unnoticed. Her chief "cause" was undoubtedly her family, but she met with the usual groups like these ladies of the Red Cross.

In 1982 Mrs. Reagan's travels took us across the United States several times. Her objective was to learn by visiting treatment centers and observing why some young people became addicts and how others could be stopped from ruining their lives. She did a lot of listening that year. She always asked the kids what they thought she as a First Lady, with a tremendous national platform, could do. They always shouted that she should work harder and harder to get the message out — a message that eventually became the slogan "Just Say No" to drugs.

As her efforts to curb drugs picked up so did the demonstrations by prodrug forces against her cause. NORML, the national marijuana lobby, often met us at the front steps of the schools and treatment centers we visited. At first Mrs. Reagan felt the demonstrations were against her personally but eventually she began to see that they were aimed at what she was trying to accomplish.

Nothing affected us on the staff like the visits to Straight, Inc., Phoenix House, Cennikor, Daytop Village, Second Genesis, and other rehabilitation programs. When you hear a child tell how she has prostituted herself or burned herself or hurt her parents and brothers and sisters just to get drugs to continue her habit, something turns inside you. Drugs, we discovered, were everywhere and everyone, regardless of income level, race or family background, was susceptible.

That year of travel, 55,000 miles in all, and the positive response she received, galvanized Mrs. Reagan's commitment to work even harder on her cause. But during 1982 we also realized that by traveling to specific locations — no matter how ambitious our schedule — she could not spread the word fast enough to reach the millions who needed to hear that drugs destroy.

So in 1983 the First Lady took to television. She appeared on an episode of the sitcom

Nancy Reagan appears with Gary Coleman in an episode of Diff'rent Strokes. *The producers of the TV show invited her to appear as herself delivering an anti-drug message to the family.*

"Diff'rent Strokes," on "Good Morning America," "Hour Magazine," and many other talk shows; she was host of a two-hour public television special called "The Chemical People." This show, designed to play at two thousand town meetings across the country, resulted in the largest grassroots movement ever to address a specific social problem. The thousands of individuals who watched, eventually organized themselves into more than five thousand local parents' groups, actually chapters of the National Federation of Parents Against Drug Abuse. Following this Democratic Congressman Charles E. Bennett introduced the National Drug Abuse Education Week bill in the House and in so doing commented, "If the first family accomplished nothing else. . . this fight against drug abuse would justify the leadership of the President and Mrs. Reagan."

In tandem with Mrs. Reagan's efforts to promote drug education and prevention, the President and his staff were working on federal drug policy which included stepped up interdiction, antigrowing and crop-elimination campaigns, expanded juvenile justice programs, and other measures. Dr. Carlton Turner, the President's advisor on drugs, often briefed Mrs. Reagan on various aspects of the problem. Mrs. Reagan carefully avoided involvement in federal legislation or government policy. She would often answer a question about her husband's policies in this area with "He is doing all he can to step up interdiction and improve the criminal justice system." While this answer frustrated reporters, in retrospect the question may have been a trap to make a First Lady seem responsible for influencing presidential policy. She knew enough not to go down that path.

I remember receiving a call from Congressman Michael Barnes, a political adversary of the Reagan Administration, who encouraged Mrs. Reagan to accept his invitation to testify at a congressional hearing on drugs. She would have nothing to do with it. Her efforts, she said, were to step up private-sector involvement and that's why she always responded to queries about increasing federal dollars for rehabilitation with

"money doesn't buy love and commitment." That's what she said she was campaigning for and what was needed most. No one cued her to take this approach, it was instinctive. Some argued she should take her case to the Congress as Congressman Barnes suggested but she felt starting down the road of involvement with the government was the wrong direction.

By 1984 it was clear that Mrs. Reagan needed to enlist others in her campaign. We turned to national service organizations like the Kiwanis, Rotary, and Lions Club. The First Lady addressed thousands of enthusiastic club members at their annual conventions. During 1984 Mrs. Reagan also called upon professional sports organizations to do more to clean up the playing field and to support the cause. Because so many sports figures came forward with their support, an annual White House tennis tournament was initiated. Proceeds from the day-long pro-am celebrity tournament were donated to the newly created Nancy Reagan Drug Abuse Foundation, an "advised" fund set up under the management of the Greater Washington Community Foundation. The fund began in 1984 to make contributions to drug treatment centers.

Another movement was started during a 1984 trip to Oakland where Mrs. Reagan was honored at a fund raiser for the Pros For Kids group. Visiting the Kennedy Elementary School, Mrs. Reagan asked the assembled children how they should respond when a pusher tried to sell them drugs. "Just say no," they responded, louder and louder. The Just Say No theme caught on and thousands of Just Say No clubs have been organized to fight drugs at the peer level.

On every foreign trip she has taken Mrs. Reagan has tried to visit drug centers or at least talk to her counterparts about the worldwide spread of drugs. She noticed, too, that when she met with other first ladies in the United States, they often asked about her drug campaign. She thought, "Why not invite other first ladies here for a meeting on the issue?" This desire became a historic two-day meeting of eighteen first ladies from around the world. What they talked about was sometimes political but always emotional.

On the first day, meeting in the East Room of the White House, they were briefed by experts and exchanged views. On the second day, they flew to Atlanta to attend and be recognized at the international meeting of PRIDE.

The first ladies' meeting led to requests for a follow-up meeting. So in the fall of 1985, Mrs. Reagan decided to hold a similar meeting at the United Nations as a part of its fortieth anniversary celebration. The meeting in the ECOSOC chamber was a first for the United Nations and cemented the feeling that if first ladies around the world united on a special cause they could have a serious impact. Despite the obvious political differences of participants that included Rosario Murillo, wife of Nicaraguan President Daniel Ortega, and Mrs. Andreas Papandreou, wife of the prime minister of Greece, a feeling of friendship emerged in the meeting.

As causes go, the elimination of drug abuse is one of the more serious ones to be undertaken by an American First Lady. Building on the record of their predecessors, future First Ladies will possibly undertake equally serious or perhaps even more monumental tasks. The more comfortable they feel with the issue and the more genuine their concern the more successful they will be.

Could Nancy Reagan have accomplished more to help solve this problem? Possibly. But she took a modest, realistic approach. She never pretended that she was a drug expert nor did she ever imply she could solve the problem or wipe out its effects. While she has already been credited with drawing national attention to this problem and its potential solutions, history will ultimately judge how well she championed her cause.

Visiting with third-graders, Mrs. Reagan was surprised by their exposure to and awareness of the drug culture. Focusing national attention on this problem prompted other organizations to take up the cause.

Political Partner

*S*arah and James Polk functioned as a unique political couple. She helped him with his speeches, correspondence, read and sifted through the newspapers and gave him advice — but always quietly, behind the scenes.

Most First Ladies have been reluctant participants in the political process. Many have abhorred it. A few refused to play any political role. Others rose on their own to the political responsibilities thrust upon them and showed themselves to be quick learners of the art of negotiation. Ultimately, a vast majority of these reluctant ladies had to assume a political role because it was dictated by their husbands' political careers or necessary to fulfill the demands of the presidency.

Many early Presidents completely ruled out

*C*hief Justice Warren Burger swears in Ronald Reagan as President in 1981 as Mrs. Reagan holds the Reagan family Bible. This custom was initiated by Lady Bird Johnson in 1965.

involvement in politics by their spouses. It was Thomas Jefferson, a man who at one time gave up national politics to devote himself to the care of his children and ailing wife, who wrote, "The tender breasts of ladies were not formed for political convulsions and the French ladies miscalculate much their own happiness when they wander from the field of their influence into that of politics."

The degree to which First Ladies have become knowledgeable about and involved in political issues largely reflects the general change in society's attitudes toward women. And as women have become more knowledgeable their outward or obvious participation in politics has become more acceptable. Even the degree to which women provided political counsel to their husbands in the privacy of their own quarters has evolved over history.

A few of the early First Ladies were both politically savvy and bold enough to seek an outlet for their opinions. In some cases this took the form of direct lobbying. Notable examples of such First Ladies are Abigail Adams, Sarah Polk, Mary Todd Lincoln, and Helen Taft.

Abigail Adams was in every respect her husband's political partner at a time when women were not expected to meddle in men's affairs. During the American Revolution, while her husband was helping to draft the Declaration of Independence, she strongly advised him to "remember the ladies" in the document and suggested some clauses that would have granted equal rights to women. While he was in Europe as a diplomat, Abigail reported to him regularly on the political climate, opinions, public movements, and elections at home. This communication on public issues continued throughout his presidency, 1779 to 1801. Abigail mistrusted the opposition, led by Thomas Jefferson, to her husband's party, the Federalists. She equally doubted the motives of the more radical element

*D*olley Madison often watched the proceedings of Congress. Here she sits in the Senate gallery (below the chandelier). In 1844, the House of Representatives granted her a seat in its Hall. (overleaf)

in Adams's own party, led by Alexander Hamilton. In fact she was at times so political and so public about her opinions that anti-Federalist Congressman Albert Gallatin dubbed her "Mrs. President."

Sarah Polk was also her husband's political partner. As his most trusted advisor, Sarah was privy to government secrets and maneuverings, and her letters reveal her to be a ruthless politician. Mrs. Polk served in a unique way by working as the President's secretary and assistant. Each morning she read through the many national newspapers the White House received and marked which editorials she felt he should read, placing them on a chair outside his office. Just as Abigail Adams was unable to convince her husband he should create a law that would give equal rights to women, Sarah was unsuccessful in her efforts to convince James Polk of the need for a national banking system. Many years later, in looking back at her tenure as First Lady, she admitted "taking a deep interest in state and national affairs."

Mary Todd Lincoln seemed to feel that playing politics was her right; and she did so without restraint. Her particular interest was personnel — both political and military. She was a good gauge of Cabinet members — like Secretary of the Treasury Salmon P. Chase, who was jealous of the President and secretly maneuvering to run against him in the 1864 election. She also disliked certain Union generals. She considered McClellan weak and Ulysses S. Grant "a butcher." Because Abraham Lincoln was so completely involved in the war, he had little time for his wife's advice. On one occasion he sarcastically remarked that perhaps, considering her self-confidence and tactical suggestions, he should place her in charge of the northern troops.

All Helen Taft would admit to was "taking an active interest in my husband's career." Mrs. Taft had steered her husband away from a career as a judge and pushed him towards the Presidency. When President Theodore Roosevelt offered William Howard Taft a position on the Supreme Court, Mrs. Taft strongly advised against it. When Roosevelt told her that Taft

would have to show some interest in pursuing the Republican nomination of 1908, it was Helen who cajoled Roosevelt into supporting Taft. On his inauguration day, she broke a precedent by riding with her husband to the White House after he was sworn in — thereby establishing a new tradition for her successors. Unfortunately, only a few months after becoming First Lady, she suffered a serious stroke which made her political role less active for much of the Taft Administration.

Starting at the image level, throughout history presidential wives have been expected to stand by their husbands, to support them and lend solidarity to the political mystique. Political couples are partly genuine and partly a creation of image makers for political consumption. A presidential candidate who appears to lack a strong marriage and family life has always been

*M*ary Lincoln nods to Secretary of the Treasury, Salmon P. Chase and his ambitious daughter, Kate, at a reception *in 1862. She felt Lincoln needed to be warned against those she thought were taking advantage of him.*

handicapped. Voters want to idealize the first couple and their marriage. They don't want to hear that the spouses have separate lives or that either has been unfaithful. In short the American people want in their first political couple things they often lack in their own marriages.

"Complete with wife" is the perfect political image and most wives of presidential candidates have been willing to support the political aspirations of their husbands. In recent history Bess Truman, Mamie Eisenhower, and Jacqueline Kennedy are remembered for their reluctance to be a part of presidential campaigns. Nevertheless they were usually on hand to complete the picture. Edith Wilson, Eleanor Roosevelt, Betty Ford, Rosalynn Carter, and

Nancy Reagan are among the more politically active First Ladies of this century.

Edith Wilson would never admit to serving as "Mrs. President," the charge she faced from many Senators after her husband suffered a stroke that left him partially paralyzed and she became the sole link to politicians clamoring to meet with him. She referred to the period as her "stewardship" and claimed that she never made a political decision on her own; but she did decide what state documents were important enough for the President to see. Mrs. Wilson claimed that she acted, not out of any reluctance to yield power, but rather to protect her husband and see he recuperated fully without unnecessary distractions. Despite her modest description of her

role, it seems clear that Mrs. Wilson was significantly involved in making decisions that directly affected government policy. Of course, the Constitution provided other options; but it is not clear that she was fully aware of these or of the potentially far-reaching implications of her involvement. Certainly, the prerogative and primary responsibility of any wife is to protect the health and well-being of her husband; but safeguards should have been exercised to assure that policy decisions were the responsibility of competent government officials. By virtue of her proximity to the most powerful position in the world, any First Lady is more than a disinterested bystander — but a government official she is not.

Eleanor Roosevelt was the most publicly political First Lady in history. She attended government conferences, inspected federal facilities, reviewed legislation, and held her own meetings with Cabinet members, union leaders, and congressmen. Because Franklin Roosevelt was physically incapacitated, his travel around the depression-ridden nation was limited. Mrs. Roosevelt served as his eyes and ears and she consciously developed the role of representative of the President. Upon her return from inspections or meetings, she fully reported the details to the President, apparently adding her own opinions about people and programs.

Eleanor Roosevelt clearly held a position which few other First Ladies have occupied. While she was openly criticized for her activism, she also mirrored women's roles in society, especially during the post-Depression and war years. The country was hard at work rebuilding the economy and supporting the war effort overseas. Women were thrust into nontraditional roles. Therefore, it didn't seem entirely unusual to the public that Mrs. Roosevelt filled roles previously held by male government officials.

The difference in the political involvement

*R*iding with her husband after his inauguration, Helen Taft sets a precedent. She had long sought the presidency for her husband, though he would have preferred a place on the Supreme Court.

of Edith Wilson and Mrs. Roosevelt was pronounced. President Wilson's stroke had impaired both his mental and physical faculties permitting judgment calls to fall to his First Lady whereas Eleanor Roosevelt only collected information to assist an able and mentally vigorous F.D.R. in making decisions. She could suggest, but dared not make decisions for him. To some degree, this latter kind of partnership has been evidenced by the activities of Betty Ford, Rosalynn Carter, and Nancy Reagan.

Betty Ford was reluctant at first, but eventually discussed political issues quite openly. She tackled questions about legalization of marijuana, the Supreme Court decision on federal funding of abortion, and the Equal Rights Amendment. Mrs. Ford admitted to changing her husband's stand on the E.R.A. and fought publicly for its national ratification. She personally lobbied representatives of states that had not yet voted for ratification of the amendment. She became the first First Lady to be publicly picketed for political outspokenness. However,

*M*any accused Edith Wilson of acting as "Mrs. President" after her husband suffered a stroke. She said she was merely protecting his health. Here she helps him sign a document; his left hand was paralyzed.

With a sad looking family standing behind her in the White House press room, Betty Ford reads her husband's concession speech. President Ford had developed laryngitis in the last few days of the campaign.

aside from her public position on issues, her political involvement was not extensive. She distinguished herself more for her candor and forthrightness about her own health problems than for any far-reaching political activity. Had she been a tenant in the White House longer, this may have not been the case.

Rosalynn Carter was a thoroughly political First Lady who was treated as an equal political partner by the President. They had weekly working luncheons. Mrs. Carter is remembered for having attended Cabinet meetings and being briefed by State Department officials before her diplomatic missions to South and Central America. She herself admitted to being part of a coup that displaced several Cabinet members midway through the Carter Administration. During the hostage crisis while the President remained working in the White House, Mrs. Carter filled in at many of his 1980 campaign appearances. Mrs. Carter had keen political antennae and an acute sense of public perception which complemented her husband's more relaxed style.

It has often been written that Nancy Reagan

and her father Dr. Loyal Davis were responsible for Ronald Reagan's conservative political ideology and his switch of party affiliation in the 1950s. This is a dramatic overstatement. True, Dr. Davis held staunchly conservative views and was a strict disciplinarian; but while he undoubtedly shared his views with his son-in-law, neither he nor Mrs. Reagan imposed strong political opinions on Mr. Reagan during the early years of their marriage. Nancy Reagan was too involved in a film career, raising a family, and developing a good marriage to concern herself, to a great extent, with politics.

Would Ronald Reagan have sought the presidency or achieved it without Nancy Reagan? Some observers credit Nancy Reagan with developing the political ambition that led her husband to become President. Again overstatement, or perhaps a misreading of the relationship. The real story of Ronald Reagan's move into politics was at the urging of friends at a time of a Republican leadership vacuum in California politics and this is well documented.

Nancy Reagan became interested in politics

only because her husband's career developed in that direction. What if Ronald Reagan's career had gone in another direction? Had he stayed in pictures, for example, Jimmy Stewart thinks that Nancy Reagan would have worked hard to see that her man got better and better parts and ultimately an Oscar. Whatever his career path, Nancy Reagan would have been her husband's prime cheerleader. She didn't choose his career for him, however.

Nancy Reagan's ambition did focus on her husband however. If she had an obsession, it would have been to be a perfect wife, to play the supporting role to perfection. She met a good match in Ronald Reagan, a man with a firm sense of values, political ideology, and commitment. What emerged in their partnership was total devotion to each other while maintaining a strong degree of individuality. Neither has dominated the other. I argue that Ronald Reagan would never have reached out to achieve the presidency had Nancy Reagan ruled the day alone. The political strategy which brought him to the White House was 50 percent his own, 25 percent from his friends and advisors, and 25 percent from Nancy Reagan.

In the 1976 and 1980 presidential campaigns Mrs. Reagan was often present at strategy meetings involving her husband, occasionally adding her own opinions. Sometimes she would seek an individual political advisor's support for a direction she felt her husband should take. Her motivation for this was not so much in terms of party platform or public issues as to ensure that her husband would succeed in his campaign. Such moves may have come out of her own drive for success in whatever she did, a built-in desire to achieve. A healthy degree of political competitiveness (but not toward each other) entered in as well, and this probably contributed to their success as a couple in politics.

Rosalynn Carter and Nancy Reagan were both far from reluctant political partners. They encouraged their candidate husbands and were their strongest supporters. I don't think either woman had any political ambition of her own — just a total devotion to her husband's goals. It was

*H*er staff joins with Mrs. Reagan to celebrate the last solo leg of the presidential election in 1984. She had become a rugged campaigner, and was much more comfortable giving speeches than in 1976 and 1980.

rumored though, after the Carters' departure from Washington that it was Rosalynn who wanted to seek elective office. Nancy Reagan's political interests could never be translated in the same way.

Rosalynn Carter probably came closest in comparison to Eleanor Roosevelt's involvement in her own political issues; both women were criticized for it. In fact, had Eleanor Roosevelt been subjected to the same scrutiny that Mrs. Carter endured, she may have been remembered differently. To the public Rosalynn Carter appeared to step too far into areas of her own

*E*leanor Roosevelt, the first First Lady to testify before members of Congress, appears before the House District Committee. She criticized conditions in three District of Columbia welfare institutions. (overleaf)

political interests, and the Carters' political advisors may have encouraged her in this. But, apparently, public opinion tolerates a degree of involvement in the President's politics while it has little toleration for the political involvement of a First Lady completely on her own.

This distinction is not lost on journalists. At the time of Donald Regan's departure as the President's chief of staff, columnists accused Nancy Reagan of being a power grabber, of trying to set her own agenda, create her own platform, and even manage the west wing and the affairs of government. Again, the critical distinction lies between a First Lady's involvement in her husband's politics and her own. Nancy Reagan was accused of pursuing her own political agenda — albeit for the benefit of her husband. There was little doubt that the First Lady wanted Don Regan out — but so did a lot of others, including the media. While Mrs. Reagan must have been

pressing for Regan's ouster in her own way, should she get all the blame, or the credit? Her interest lay in having effective people serve her husband. According to many people, Don Regan had outlived his usefulness.

During this time, several things occurred to me which argue against the indictment that Nancy Reagan was grabbing the reins of government. First, Mrs. Reagan had a track record in running a domestic social program, the drug abuse campaign, in which she repeatedly refused — sometimes against the staff's recommendations — to integrate into the President's drug policy or any government program. She never sought government money to fight drugs, attended only one meeting in the west wing on drug policy, refused an invitation to testify before Congress, and insisted on keeping her efforts totally oriented toward the private sector. Often it seemed logical to her staff that she merge

A working lunch in the President's private office every Thursday (such as this one in 1979) helped Jimmy and Rosalynn Carter cope with joint concerns of politics and official life.

*April 15, 1969, finds Mrs. Nixon beside her husband at an unprecedented session of the Cabinet. It was the first
meeting ever attended by a First Lady and Cabinet wives. The group remained throughout the proceedings.*

her efforts with the work of government offices. She refused to be a government spokesman. Although many groups pressured her to seek increased government spending for this problem, she said her role was to increase awareness, not spending. She had ample opportunity to create her own political power from this crusade but she resisted it.

Another example of her lack of interest in a personal political agenda was shown in her trip to earthquake-torn Mexico City. She was asked to go there as the official representative of the President, or of the American people. But she set her own terms: she went as a private citizen, a friend of the Mexican people. She said that she went to extend a hand of friendship.

Nancy Reagan eventually overcame a lack of confidence in speaking publicly to become a successful campaigner. In 1976 and 1980 she rarely campaigned apart from her husband. By the time 1984 came around, she crisscrossed the country several times integrating meetings on drug abuse at many stops. The public saw a

different Nancy Reagan than that of her first two years in the White House. She was always quick to pick up on support, or lack of it, for her husband; and she addressed problems or pointed them out to the campaign staff. At the end of every campaign day, she would head for the telephone to share her perceptions about issues and voters' concerns with the top advisors for her husband's campaign. After the first presidential debate in 1984, she felt that advisors had not prepared the President sufficiently. She stepped in to suggest a new approach, but she never participated specifically in debate preparation beyond the level of pointed suggestions.

How much political power does a First Lady really have? In any political situation the perception of power may be as important as the actual ability to effect change. A President's wife attains her position through marriage. Public trust has not been placed in her through the process of election or appointment. No accountability process, except perhaps consensus reached through public debate, covers the presidential spouse.

*N*ancy Reagan inspects earthquake-torn Mexico City
accompanied by Mrs. de la Madrid, Mexico's First
Lady, and United States Ambassador John Gavin. She
made the trip as a private citizen.

She does not figure in the carefully thought out
order of succession should the President become
unavailable to serve. Although she may be more
familiar with the demands of the job and the
President's agenda than others who might assume
the presidential duties, the Constitution does
not accord her privilege or responsibility. Because of legal constraints, any First Lady must
be cautious about exercising the political power
she could easily tap. If the proximity to power can
be equated to the ability to influence, any First
Lady could be considered the second most
powerful person in the country. To date, no First
Lady has seriously abused this privilege.

I distinctly remember the days at the
Bethesda Naval Hospital during the President's
first cancer surgery. The First Lady held a
constant vigil over the President's mental and
physical well-being. Although she could have
easily integrated herself into the affairs of government, she made no move to usurp the responsibilities of the staff. She had her opinion about
recovery time and rest, but she showed no
interest in being a surrogate President or even a
presidential advisor. She was too busy answering
the hundreds of calls from family and friends
around the world. Also, I think the President
would have been very uncomfortable with relin-
quishing responsibility to anyone. Clearly, opportunities exist to seize power and future First
Ladies will have to guard against the temptation
to abuse their position.

Politics is a realm that a First Lady enters by
default. Millions judge her performance and it is
a difficult position to be in. There are no
definitive standards to be judged against and
public opinion determines her grade.

*E*nthusiastic supporters wave their flags as the Reagan family gathers for their portrait after the 1984 election. This
was only two days after Mrs. Reagan had suffered a fall from a platform bed at a Sacramento hotel.

Wife & Mother

For the thirty-eight presidents who have called the White House home, and for their wives and families, it has been mostly a bittersweet tenure. Ronald Reagan has referred to life in the White House as "living above the store." Franklin Roosevelt said it was like being on "public display;" and the recalcitrant Harry Truman labeled it as being in "a great white prison." Most first families have tried to get away from the mansion and its grounds for brief periods — especially during the hot Washington summers before air conditioning. Thomas Jefferson returned to his favorite summer retreat, Poplar Forest, near Lynchburg, Virginia. Grover Cleveland built a summer cottage on a hilltop three miles north of the White House to catch the few summer breezes that pass through the muggy capital. Herbert Hoover escaped to a camp in the Blue Ridge Mountains for his favorite pastime, fishing. Franklin Roosevelt frequented Warm Springs, Georgia, and also established a presidential retreat in the Catoctin Mountains of Maryland, now known as Camp David. Successive Presidents have enjoyed weekends and holidays there. Other first families chose different getaways. The Kennedys preferred Hyannis Port, Newport, or the Virginia hunt country, while President Nixon spent his vacations in either Florida or California.

For all First Families there has been the glare of the spotlight and the constant criticism of the public. A circle of family and friends, pulled close amidst the clamor, becomes a buffer to the pressure of the job and a necessary tonic.

Twelve Presidents had children attending grammar or high school while living with them in the White House. Sixteen presidential families counted among their clans grandchildren who played in the house and grounds at 1600 Pennsylvania Avenue. Some grandchildren lived in the house for full presidential tenures and others made extended visits.

Ron Reagan and his mother take a spin around the White House grounds on a bicycle built for two. The Reagans have never been able to satisfy the public's insatiable desire for information about their children.

Standing outside their Philadelphia house, George Washington and Nellie Custis, Martha's granddaughter, welcome news from Mount Vernon. Martha's activities were largely limited to domestic family needs.

Thomas Jefferson's daughter Martha bore the first child in the White House. Martha Washington's two grandchildren, Nellie and "Little Wash," lived with the First Lady in successive presidential mansions in New York and Philadelphia. When Herbert and Lou Hoover's son was taken ill, the couple took his children to live at the White House while their father recuperated. Once young Peter Hoover surprised a crowd on the lawn by appearing in the buff at an upstairs window. The Franklin Roosevelt's grandchildren by their daughter Anna also lived at the White House in the early F.D.R. years. "Sistie" and "Buzzie" Dall amused the nation

Jacqueline Kennedy escorts a buggy full of Kennedy-clan children in Hyannis Port, the family retreat. The youngest first lady in this century, she had come to the White House with two young children. (overleaf)

*L*eaving the East Room where they had just exchanged vows, Linda Bird Johnson and Captain Charles Robb walk beneath an arch of cross swords. Only 14 months earlier, Linda had caught sister Luci's wedding bouquet.

with their antics on a swing set installed by their grandmother on the White House lawn. Similarly Amy Carter's treehouse attracted attention in 1977. The Eisenhower grandchildren delighted the press and public — from a granddaughter's christening in the Blue Room to David's earnest emulation of his grandfather.

Other relatives have come to live with their kin at the White House. Julia Grant's father, a staunch Confederate, often voiced his political differences with his son-in-law, the general who had a few short years earlier defeated the rebels. Caroline Harrison's niece Mary Lord Dimmick served as her aunt's assistant and, by a strange quirk of history, married President Harrison after her aunt Caroline died. Mary Todd Lincoln's sister Emily, the widow of a Confederate soldier, was welcomed with open arms by President Lincoln. He knew her presence would calm his wife's delicate mental state in the period after the Lincoln son Willie died. Franklin Delano Roosevelt's dominant and often testy mother, Sara,

came for extended stays at the White House. When she began instructing the mansion's staff on how to do things, the First Lady pulled her confidence together and told her mother-in-law off. "Mother, you run your house, I'll run mine."

The White House has been the scene of a few illustrious weddings; always family occasions, these became international events. The wedding of President Grover Cleveland to his young ward Frances Folsom merited worldwide attention. In the city of Washington, the press reported around the clock on even the most insignificant of the bride's activities. At the magic moment, with crowds pressed up against the windows of the mansion, all of Washington's bells pealed, cannons boomed, and whistles were blown. Alice Roosevelt's wedding to Nicholas Longworth brought forth a torrent of presents — from a barrel of popcorn to ancient vases from the empress of China. Songs were written for the occasion and sheet music featured a picture of the bride. In contrast a comedy album was cut spoofing the grand arrangements made for Luci Johnson's wedding to Patrick Nugent at the Shrine of the Immaculate Conception in Washington and the reception which followed at the White House.

Although few of the White House children have earned honors on their own, all have been the focus of attention. Alice Roosevelt entered the spotlight as a difficult child. She marched to her own drummer and thrived on the public attention. When Margaret Truman attempted to pursue a career in opera, she became open game for reporters. After a particularly disparaging review, President Truman threatened to punch the author for criticizing "the apple of my eye." Caroline Kennedy was the center of national attention although her mother attempted to protect her from the scrutiny of a curious press and public. Caroline's every word merited a story; her White House nursery school activities were reported with as much interest as were her mother's activities. Jack and Susan Ford, who lived in the White House, also drew media attention. Jack's political opinions, which sometimes differed from his father's, and Susan's high-school prom, held in the East Room, found their way into the weekly newsmagazines. Even their brother Steve's motorcycle and rodeo escapades were covered. Very few First Ladies have been required to provide mothering to small children while performing official duties. And many of the older children have had a nagging feeling that they came a distant second in line for their mother's attention when she was serving as First Lady.

Jacqueline Kennedy said that the most important role she would play as First Lady was that of wife and mother, adding that if one didn't do well in those roles then no other role really mattered. She held up Bess Truman as the First Lady she most admired because Bess had managed to raise a teenage daughter in the glare of publicity at a time when a young woman's life was difficult enough without that.

Most other First Ladies have shared that view. Indeed, Bess Truman guarded her private relationship with the President and Margaret so

vehemently that they were dubbed "The Three Musketeers" by the household staff. The Trumans were formal in public, but affectionate in private. Once, the morning after the First Lady returned from a long trip, she embarrassingly made a request of the chief usher: the slats of the presidential bed had broken in the night and needed to be replaced.

Lady Bird Johnson told the White House staff on her very first day that her husband's needs come first, her daughters' needs came second, and she, herself, came last. Though Lyndon Johnson could be a tyrant to work for and live with, Lady Bird could manage him — soothe his temper and then smooth the feathers he ruffled. The President often remarked that he owed everything to his wife. Jacqueline Kennedy, during the 1960 campaign remarked on this loyalty, noting how Mrs. Johnson followed her husband with a note pad and pencil writing down questions he needed answers to and listing people to call and arrangements to be made.

*M*argaret Truman sings a duet with opera star Ezio Pinza. A singing career was derailed by the glare of press scrutiny. Margaret was an only child and the family was a particularly close and devoted one.

Whenever travel took her away from her two daughters, Luci and Lynda, Mrs. Johnson always ended her telephone conversations with them with the gentle remark, "Just remember, you are loved."

Rosalynn Carter had a similar relationship with her husband. They were partners in every sense of the word — publicly and privately. They jogged and exercised together, took Spanish lessons together, and even arranged a weekly luncheon for just the two of them. Abigail and John Adams shared a similar intimacy. President Adams called his wife "My dearest friend," and their love letters — intermixed with political opinions, information and secrets — total in the thousands. The Adamses were apart the majority of his one term as President and the First Lady kept him intimately informed on the lives of their four children. John Quincy, who later became President himself, was serving in various diplo-

Lady Bird Johnson finds time in her busy schedule to hear Lynda tell of her vacation trip through the West in 1965 and to see her pictures. They gathered in Lynda's younger sister, Luci's, White House bedroom.

matic posts and remained particularly close to his mother through a constant stream of letters. Still, he went ahead and married the English-born Louisa Catherine Johnson against Abigail's advice. Charles, another Adams son, an alcoholic, was dying when his mother was leaving for the new capital. She made one last painful visit to him in November 1800. Into the newly built presidential mansion in Washington, she took a granddaughter Suzanna; and the President and First Lady cherished her presence in the lovely cold house.

Eleanor and Franklin Roosevelt had a partnership of a different sort. By the time they entered the White House in 1933, passion had

Susan Ford, at right, entertains members of her high school class at the first senior prom ever held at the White House. She had previously served as hostess during her mother's recovery from breast cancer surgery.

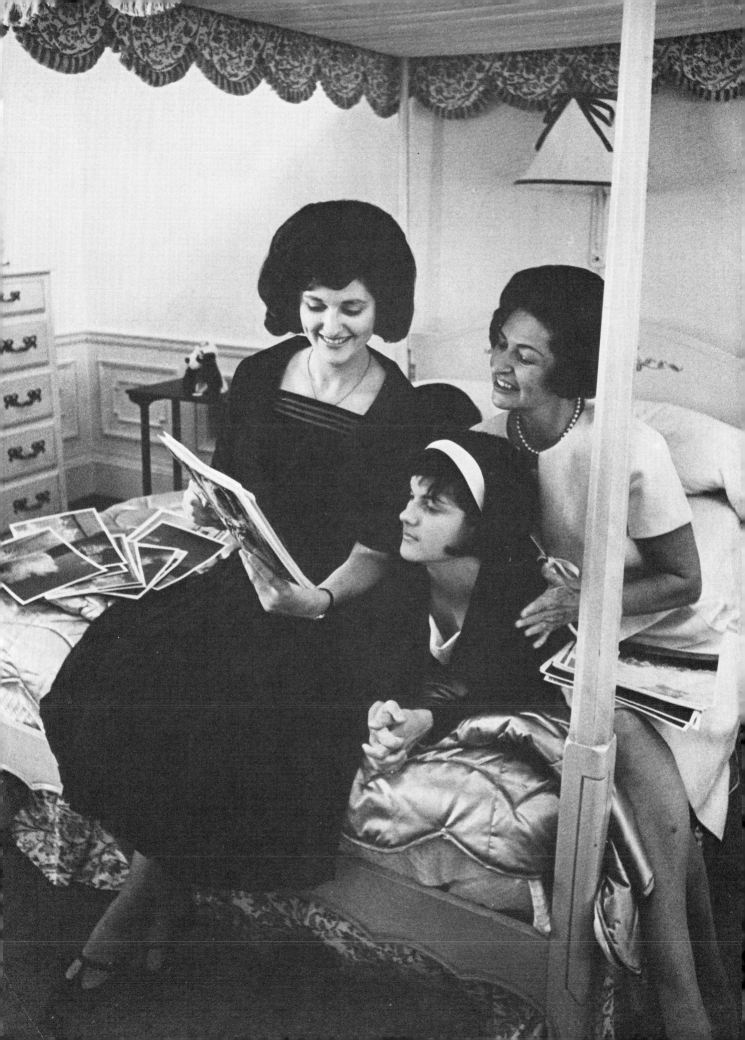

*P*resident and Mrs. Franklin Roosevelt, upstaged by their thirteen grandchildren, pose on the occasion of his unique fourth inaugural. They formed the largest number of grandchildren ever assembled at the White House.

long since left the couple, but not mutual respect. Their unique arrangement allowed Eleanor total freedom to work on her husband's projects and her own. They frequently traveled separately and each kept a rigorous individual schedule. When, one morning, the President was told that Eleanor "was in prison," he joked, "I'm not surprised. What's she in for?" Family gatherings at Christmas and Thanksgiving found Eleanor and Franklin together, surrounded by their large clan of children, grandchildren, great-aunts, cousins, nephews, and nieces. Though her children may have had to compete with her public schedule to discuss serious things with her, Eleanor Roosevelt made room for her grandchildren in her hectic life.

Marital bliss has not always prevailed at 1600 Pennsylvania Avenue, Louisa Adams resented being pushed into the background, and often marched away to her room, angry at her husband. Mary Todd Lincoln threw temper tantrums when things didn't go as she wished; and the President, frustrated with the realities of the Civil War, had to manage his own bouts of depression while gently coaxing his wife out of her extreme mood swings. Jane Pierce was so angered when she discovered that her husband had lied to her when he said he had not actively

pursued the presidency, that she steadfastly refused to attend his inauguration, getting off of the train at Baltimore and staying there. A personal visit and appeal by President-elect Pierce could not move her.

Florence and Warren Harding's fights were notorious. President Harding often sneaked out of the house to visit one of his mistresses, and "The Duchess" put up a fight every time. "You're not leaving this house tonight!" she shouted to him one evening over the banister in full view of the servants. His wandering eye for young women angered the First Lady so that she even admonished him in front of reporters. When the Hardings weren't speaking to each other, they often spoke through to their airedale Laddie Boy, telling him to tell the other something. President Harding once confessed that his wife was "a good scout" who knew his faults and still put up with him.

Children were sometimes the cause of marital strife in the White House. The crazy antics of Alice Roosevelt often shocked her

*G*uests crowd into the White House for the wedding of Theodore Roosevelt's daughter Alice — dubbed "Princess Alice" by the press — to Nicholas Longworth. Alice enjoyed a seven-decade reign in social Washington.

stepmother, Edith, who reported things to her husband. President Roosevelt once told someone else who complained about Alice, "I can do one of two things, I can run the country or control Alice. I cannot do both."

The Reagans have never been able to satisfy the insatiable desire for gossip or just plain information about their children. When they entered the White House, all four children — Maureen, Michael, Patti, and Ron — were grown and establishing careers, mostly in California. Their leading separate lives prompted many to conclude that they did not support their parents. It may have been especially important for Ron and Patti to establish independence, and they chose to do this, to the extent possible, away from the glare of the White House. On many occasions I witnessed warm exchanges between

the Reagans' children and their parents; but theirs was a very private relationship. Mrs. Reagan often interrupted a staff meeting or other small gathering to take a phone call from her children. I never heard a complaint from anyone on the staff about these interruptions. Everyone understood the importance of her role as mother.

The situation with Michael and Maureen was more public. Mike, by nature, was more vocal; and several misunderstandings developed over what Mike and his parents allegedly said publicly about each other. Finally, through direct communications, they worked out their differences. Maureen has become closer and closer to the Reagans during their years in the White House. This coincided with Maureen's involvement in Republican politics. Her work at the Republican National Committee brought her to Washington frequently so she was a regular guest at the White House. Maureen provided a natural support group of one as well as a family sounding board. After all, she knew the political situations facing her father and she could share her knowledgeable opinions with the Reagans. And opinions she had! This gave Maureen broad appeal to the public. She became the natural focus for the unsatisfied public interest in Reagan family opinions. She is not afraid to say what she thinks about tough political issues and she is a free agent. She sets forth her own views and she shows the Reagans to be a family not unlike other American families.

Whether we agree with their politics or not, the style, temperaments, sorrows, successes, and failures of presidential families subtly affect our view of our own families and of the collective conscience of the nation. One of Ronald Reagan's contributions to this collective conscience was the renewal of a sense of pride in individual achievement and confidence in our democratic way of life. Had the Reagans had stronger family ties they might have provided role models in that area as well; but to expect perfection from presidential families is to invite disappointment.

Perhaps the fact that the families who occupy the White House are just a little too much like ordinary citizens both gladdens and disap-

Nancy Reagan took time out of most every day to call her mother, the former stage actress, Edith Davis. Although in failing health, Mrs. Davis maintained her sharp wit. Here they share a moment of affection.

points us. When a candidate declares for the presidency, he is declaring an open season for the inspection of his family — from the Alice Roosevelts to the Billy Carters. The public has been spared most of the details of the Reagans' parent-child relationships since communication has been largely private. The public search for family-life details has gone unsatisfied. The public had grown used to a flow of family information from the Carters, Fords, Nixons, Johnsons, and Kennedys. A measure of public interest in the Reagan family was the hundreds of requests we had for an early 1981 photo of Nancy Reagan riding a bicycle built for two with her son Ron.

In the supporting role of wife, most First Ladies have been models of tolerance, forbearance, and rugged loyalty. They have been staunch allies. Abigail Adams felt the closeness between her and her husband was crucial to weathering the criticism the Adamses would likely face. "I expect to be vilified and abused with my whole family when I come into this situation," she wrote. But she believed that she and her husband must "strictly adhere to our duty and keep ourselves unprejudiced. We may truly say, we know not what a day will bring forth. . . ." Knowing that her husband would be too busy as President to oversee their property, Mrs. Adams assumed that job herself, and managed his investments and land.

Writers often made fun of the adoring gaze with which Mrs. Reagan seems to observe her husband. Whatever the reason it must have always been important to her that her marriage last and, moreover, that it be happy. And for this alone, in an era of high divorce rates, especially in California, they must receive some credit. From the beginning, their relationship has been traditional. The many years of this marriage has shown a tremendous dedication and loyalty. It's been a match in which each partner maintained a strong individuality and character but worked to blend his outlook and activities to complement the other. As a public wife Mrs. Reagan could easily have made herself an example; but time and time again she refused to speak publicly

about marriage and family. Perhaps she sensed a degree of vulnerability; but she took a truly American stand: to try to set an example rather than preach.

The private wife may not always remain the same when she becomes the public wife. Private relationships have a way of stretching and growing — or breaking — as a result of public attention. The public allows a first couple few private relationships with each other and forgets that the public interpretation of personal behavior is rarely an adequate, or even correct, interpretation of how a couple feels about each other. The couples living in the White House have shown as many different kinds of relationships as there have been Presidents. Most seem to reflect genuine devotion. This was surely the case of the Reagans.

*T*he Reagans' 33-year love story is sealed with a kiss *and a lone candle on their anniversary cake. Nancy Reagan, who has always put her husband's needs first, has grown in her job to embrace the needs of many others.*

Acknowledgments

I wish to express my gratitude to a number of people who helped make this book possible: Mary Anne Fackelman-Miner and the entire White House photo office; First Lady historian Carl Sferrazza; editors Elizabeth Fisher and Geraldine Linder; and the design firm of Meadows & Wiser. I would also like to thank Jed Lyons and Charles Lean of Madison Books who agreed that the changing role of the First Lady in American political life is worthy of a book-length study.

Picture Credits

Page 2, 6, The White House; 8, Culver Pictures Inc.; 9 bottom, Culver Pictures Inc., top, The White House; 10, The White House; 11, Library of Congress; 12, John F. Kennedy Library; 13, Culver Pictures Inc.; 14–15, District of Columbia Public Library; 16, Gerald R. Ford Library; 17, The White House; 19, 20, Culver Pictures Inc.; 21, Lyndon B. Johnson Library; 22, The White House; 23, The Pierce Brigade, Concord, NH; 24–25, painting by Louis Glanzman, The White House Historical Assn.; 27, Culver Pictures Inc.; 28, painting by Gordon Phillips, The White House Historical Assn.; 29, Library of Congress; 30, 31, Abbie Rowe, National Park Service; 33, Ed Clark, Life Magazine © 1958 Time, Inc.; 34, 35, White House Photo; 36–37, Culver Pictures Inc.; 39, Library of Congress; 40, 43, The White House; 44, Brooklyn Public Library; 45, Culver Pictures Inc.; 47–49, The White House; 50, 51, Culver Pictures Inc.; 52–53, Cornell Capa, Magnum; 55, Library of Congress; 56–57, painting by Thomas Rossiter, Smithsonian Institution, Museum of American Art; 57, bottom, The White House; 58, UPI/Bettman News Photos; 60, Gerald R. Ford Library; 61, 62, The White House; 63, Donald Crump, National Geographic Society staff, White House Historical Assn.; 64–70, The White House; 71, Library of Congress; 72, painting by Charles Bird King, Smithsonian Institution, Museum of American Art; 73, Leet Brothers Company; 74, Donald Crump, National Geographic Society staff, White House Historical Assn.; 75 Jackie Marten, Franklin D. Roosevelt Library; 76, Art Rickerby, Life Magazine © 1963 Time, Inc.; 77, White House Photo; 78, Steve Raymer, National Geographic Society staff, White House Historical Assn.; 79, The White House; 80, 81, 82 left and center, Culver Pictures Inc.; 82 right, New York Public Library; 83, Culver Pictures Inc.; 84, The White House; 85, AP/Wide World Photos; 87, Culver Pictures Inc.; 88, Lyndon B. Johnson Library; 89–91, The White House; 92, Visiting Nurses Assn.; 93, Culver Pictures Inc.; 94, CBS; 95, Jimmy Carter Library; 96, Culver Pictures Inc.; 97–100, The White House; 101, Culver Pictures Inc.; 102–103, U.S. Capitol Collection, Architect of the Capitol; 104–105, Library of Congress; 106, Historical Pictures Service; 107, Culver Pictures Inc.; 108, Gerald R. Ford Library; 109, The White House; 110, Nelson Rimensnyder; 112, Jimmy Carter Library; 113, National Archives; 114–117, The White House; 118–119, Photo Researchers; 120, White House Historical Assn.; 121, Culver Pictures Inc.; 122, Gerald R. Ford Library; 123, Robert L. Knudsen; 124, Franklin D. Roosevelt Library; 125, White House Historical Society; 126, 127, The White House.